OTHER BOOKS BY

ALLAN KNIGHT CHALMERS

As He Passed By

Give Me Another Chance

The Commonplace Prodigal

Candles in the Wind

Candles in the Wind

BY

ALLAN KNIGHT CHALMERS

NEW YORK
CHARLES SCRIBNER'S SONS
1941

To my daughter

ELIZABETH

and

All who bear the Light

Foreword

MAN can believe most anything if he sees it done. To be sure, he is sometimes skeptical and claims it has been done with mirrors. "I wouldn't believe it if I saw it myself and had two witnesses," some one remarked to me about a certain type of spiritual reaction to life-under-pressure which I had claimed was possible for every man and woman and which he claimed was contrary to human nature. This is a common attitude of some people. They have been burned too often to believe very much in the inherent goodness of human nature. And they can shrug off anything which is just an idea.

This is the point where Christianity has failed so often. The seeming weakness of the Church is not that man has not ideals enough; nor that there are not men who will fearlessly proclaim those ideals. We fail because there is not a sufficient group of mankind holding to the ideal as the supreme motivation of life and bringing to bear on our daily existence an intelligent and effectual movement toward the goal.

It is an awareness of the need to keep the good people of the world from being contented with a religion which is satisfied to protest and proclaim but has not yet transformed the world into the "Beloved Community," which has made me write that *Candles in the Wind* are not enough to light this world.

There would be no point in saying this unless there

ix

was so much more of positive hope which can and must be said. Sharing as I do with many people a Dark Night of the Soul in which it seemed that there was no light adequate for this windy world, I have no longer a fear that the Light ever can be put out by the darkness. I have sympathy because I have been through the time of utter discouragement wherein one asks but one boon of God: that one might be let to die. Having known the experience of going through to the light again, one can never forget that after impenetrable darkness there was light—and "it was good."

This book aims at producing the feeling of belief in "the true light which lighteth every man that cometh into the world," so that from that confidence in the truth we see in Christ may come the compulsion to apply the light with intelligence and with undiminished persistence. We are in more danger from the "little faith" of the children of light than we are from all the demons of fact or fiction. I shall have hit my mark if you feel, when you finish your reading, that you do believe you can yet find the way which you and the world need.

ALLAN KNIGHT CHALMERS

Broadway Tabernacle Church
    New York City
        January, 1941

Contents

Candles in the Wind

CHAPTER ONE

And Darkness Was

THERE is an ancient symbol of which you and I are a part, and there is no way in which we can escape that fact. Religion is supposed to represent the light. It is a queer quality of life upon which one cannot always put one's finger, but it is there. Though people may sneer at religion and be sceptical about the way we call ourselves Christians, they do expect us to show something to the world—are vaguely dissatisfied when we are apparently no different from the rest of the world.

They have a right to that expectancy. After all we have claimed that there is an idea in the midst of life, and if man dares to stay near it, and will do some adventurous thinking about it, he will be caught by a splendor—a light which penetrates the frame of man's substance until he becomes "charged with the strength of flame." The last phrase, which is one Shelley tried to work into his "Ode to Liberty" and could not, is the need of the world today.

Without too much insistence at first on making everything we think about fit at once into some nicely ordered scheme of thought, let's see what this symbol of light means in our way of looking at life.

We start with a very quiet fact. Light is always superior to darkness. Darkness never blots out light. This is a very simple fact and easy to demonstrate. Light a candle and enter a dark place. Wherever the candle goes, the darkness disappears. A wind can blow the light out. It may use up the substance from which it has its being. But the darkness itself has no power over it. So long as the light burns, the darkness, in that spot, is without power. Darkness takes possession at once if the light is taken away. It seems almost sinister the way it sneaks around you and fills in where you were, the moment you take the light elsewhere. Nevertheless there is no opposite example in this world of our experience. Light is always superior to darkness. As the Christmas hymn, "Silent Night," says,

"Darkness flies, all is light."

We add the place of fire in the history of life. Crowd with me into a wet, cold lean-to against a rock on the trail, to make simple symbolism of it. We are weary and shivering and very conscious of the party of boys whom we are leading. We are trying with damp matches and wet wood to coax a fire to burn. A bit of smoke gives hope. The proverb usually means evil but this time is blessed— "There is no smoke without some fire." Beneath a grating we try to create with tired fingers a constant draft by waving a tin plate. The fire catches on. The flame transforms a shivering, miserable group of boys into a cheerful camp again. Warm food, dry clothes, unifying good cheer. A touch from a poet's appreciation of how civilization came upon the miracle of fire, says:

"He stood erect, and to an undreamed goal
    Reached, troubled by the whispering of
      thought.
Came fire at his command, a mystery brought
By moving hands and sticks. His yearning soul
Reached up a little, hid, and feared the Whole;
    Dreamed mightily, and deemed that thus was
      wrought
The last great miracle."[1]

The scene shifts. We stand suddenly in the midst of one of man's most terrifying experiences: Fire out of control. Unleashed now—fierce, irresistible. I've never been in an earthquake, though I have seen the results four days afterward. I have been under shell-fire—the longest time for twelve uninterrupted days and nights. But a forest fire beats anything I have known for the feeling of unadulterated helplessness. Ringed with flame you fight on, scarce knowing why. Your arms feel at last unable to lift a rake handle. There is no hope against such power. Your strength is gone against the strength of the flames. Then reinforcements appear in the smoke, and your dulled senses realize that you may yet bring this power under control. The sheer, bewildering strength of flame!

We draw a final picture. The Sidewalk Superintendents' Club has punched the time clock. Workmen

[1]Kathryn Peck, "Progress," in *Songs from the Silence*, the Stratford Company.

are tearing down a building. By the smashing power of a swinging steel ball they batter down brick and stone. But the steel skeleton remains. It was erected to stand the tug and pull of winds. Earthquakes will twist and bend but will not separate it. Axes will blunt their edges against it. Saws could laboriously work through it. But flame, organized effectively in man's hands, becomes a torch to draw across the steel. As a hot knife goes through butter, so this torch dismembers steel. Thus the light tears down the old.

Now to build. Can the flame help there? Man takes his new girders. He cannot jam them together and with terrific pressure make them stay. He cannot pound them into submission to his will. But he takes his flame, now differently organized, and the cold, unyielding, separate pieces become fused into one.

One is reminded of God's call to Jeremiah: "See, I have set thee over the nations and over the kingdoms to tear up and pull down and destroy—to plant and to build."

Shelley said it,

> "Within the cavern of man's troubled spirit
>   Is throned an Image, so intensely fair
> That the adventurous thoughts that wander
>   near it
>   Worship, and as they kneel, tremble—and
>   wear
> The splendor of its presence—And the light
>   Penetrates their dreamlike frame
> Till they become charged with the strength of
>   flame."[2]

[2]Literary Notes of Shelley about "Ode to Liberty."

The words of John about Jesus close our overture. "In Him was life and the life was the light of men and the light shineth in the darkness and the darkness could not blot it out. . . . And as many as received Him"—this light of life—or should we call it this life of light?—"To them gave He power to become . . . the sons and daughters of God."

There is a strength in the flame of man's spirit.

Man is not man in any significant meaning of the word when he is without hope—a transforming hope. He defeats the fog of doubt by the power of a constant fire of faith within his soul which cannot be overcome because it will not admit defeat. Man was meant for righteousness. Every man that hath this conviction in him purifieth himself, even as Christ also is pure.

There is a love that never fails. It is an affirmation. Those who do not believe it will not do anything about it. They will become as other men—running to the bombproof cells of their fear for self when the going gets tough. They are honest men and will live well enough within the limits of the life they see. They will be useless in building the Kingdom of God and of His Christ.

There will be those, and some of them will read these words, who see but cannot bear the sight. They both hurt and help the vision Christ saw so clearly. They hurt because they see and do not. They help because, when the sight haunts them with a feeling which will not let them rest, they keep the dream alive in men's minds. Something is unquiet in life until they match the real world at last to truth. But these will not build the Kingdom of God and of His Christ.

There are others who see what Jesus wants. They see—and storm and stress turn them not aside.

It is useless to stand out against wrong in such a world—so say men of that world. Not useless!

But it is impossible to change the racial prejudices of men. Black, Jew, Jap, Hun, Beast, Barbarian: the sweep of the forest fires of man's hates rises like Wagnerian music in a hopeless world. Not impossible! He never said it was easy, but He never said it was impossible.

But why should I sacrifice myself for something I shall not see? practical people say. Why? Because it is the only realism. Light stays in the world when men hold it. Remember what Latimer said to Ridley as they brought man's flames close to burn them who for conscience' sake would not be silent: "Be of good cheer, Master Ridley. We shall this day light such a candle in England as shall never be put out."

A man living in our time gave expression to our theme in a prayer. He put it into the mouth of Icarus, son of Dædalus, that mythological inventor of wings by which men first flew. It was, however, of his own life and times that he wrote. He knew he might not survive the experiment of protest. Pioneers so often fail to live. But he knew some one must point the way.

He pictures the father hesitating, as Icarus makes his prayer. The words were found among the things that remained when De Bosis, lover of democracy and hater of war, tried to keep sanity in Italy when the Black Shirts with their might came in. Speech, assembly, press, all civil rights were crushed out. But the right of life to protest with its life was not conquered.

Printing some leaflets, De Bosis took a plane and scattered them upon Rome. He sowed his seed without anxiety about what the full harvest would be. The planes of the Black Shirts went up after him, and De Bosis was never seen again. But his prayer lives.

Young Icarus stands on the edge of what men say will never be attained—because it is impossible. He prays:

"Soul of the world, Force of the cosmos, Unknown Whom we revere, this life, this heart, I offer Thee! Grant that I follow my Guardian Spirit through the sky, and equal with deeds of life, the speed of thought. Thou Who seest all things in the immeasurable sea of the future, if it must be that I fall, grant that my blood be forever fertile and live again in every age. Grant that my name be the pledge of courage, that my sons dare more than the unchanging laws allow; grant that this way to which I consecrate myself be one day the common heritage of the redeemed sons of men; and if I die, may this my death seem to the living far more beautiful than any life they know. Through me may love of great deeds burn more strongly in them; may they yearn with more ardor to vanquish all that seems forbidden to the impetuous will of man.

"O God, Eternal, I consecrate to Thee, in this day of glory, myself, and all those who, at the price of life, shall carry forward toward the Holy City the sacred flame of Thy Spirit.

"Father, bind on my wings!"[3]

We must not be fooling. Christianity has placid times, but it is a flame. There is power in it. But danger to those through whom it must work. To believe and to make yourself the channel for the love of God is more than going to church. No man can tell you what to do. Many will try, but they are not necessarily right. But there is a cost to the Kingdom. Some day you will be asked to pay your share.

[3]Lauro de Bosis, *Icarus* (trans. by Ruth Draper), pp. 151–152. Oxford University Press.

CHAPTER TWO

Candles in the Wind

ID you ever try to carry a candle in the wind? It is a very self-centering process. So self-centering that it becomes, after a while, self-defeating. You have taken the candle in your hand that its light may show you where to place your feet in the darkness. You pay no attention to the candle as you walk. Your eyes are on the turns and bumps of the path, lest you stumble.

But your candle in the wind demands attention. You cannot carry it beside you as you peer ahead in the darkness seeking out the way. It flutters and sputters. You bring it—must bring it—down in front of yourself to guard it with your hand from the wind. After a while you find that you have had to center upon it so closely that all its value is gone. You see nothing but the light and are once more a prisoner of the darkness. All your attention is taken up with guarding the flame and your feet stumble anyway. Some gusty night along a country road try to carry —a candle in the wind. But you do not need to. The experience is so obvious.

Obvious, but not applied. Think of those services of real emotional beauty, the candlelight services of

the church. I am thinking of a young people's candlelight service at one of our summer conferences. The
chaplain has made his final appeal to the young people
to consecrate life to the highest they know. Then all
the lights go out in the auditorium, save a single light
from a candle before the cross. In the hand of each
delegate is an unlighted candle.

The solemn ritual begins. The faculty move one
by one toward the cross; light their candles there;
pass down the steps through the silent dark to the
sober young people waiting in the first pews. The
light is passed from faculty to delegate. Those in the
front pew turn and in their turn pass on the light
from candle to candle and a wave of light sweeps
out of the darkness.

In the glory of the blazing lights, the conference
begins to sing:

"To the knights in the days of old,
Keeping watch on the mountain's height,
Came a vision of Holy Grail,
And a voice through the waiting night.
Follow, follow, follow the gleam. . . ."

On that line the recessional begins. With a light upon
their faces that never was on land or sea, with heads
high and faces alight as neophytes to knighthood
pass, with hands clasped around the candles as crusaders to conquests or priests to prayers, in a halo of
holiness the line marches out of the chapel singing
as they go:

"And we who would serve the King
And loyally Him obey,

In the consecrate silence know
That the challenge still holds today.

"Follow, follow, follow the gleam,
Standards of worth o'er all the earth.
Follow, follow, follow the gleam
Of the light that shall bring the dawn."[1]

In the soft summer air I have seen them go, across
the campus to room or tent, like Peter Pan's fairies
to their beds in the trees—a campus "all lit for mar-
vels." Behind each light a life, on every lip a prayer—
a prayer that life shall be never as it was; from now
on ever at the highest.

Taps sound:

"Day is done,
Gone the sun,
From the hill, from the lake, from the sky,
All is well,
Safely rest,
God is nigh."

The lights go out and the campus is dark with a
sense of completion.

". . . We have come at last
To that still center where the spinning world
Sleeps on its axis. . . ."

This is the plan and this sometimes the way it
worked. But tonight a wind is blowing. As they come
out to the chapel steps, heads high, hearts holy—puff,
the light is gone. It is almost ludicrous to see the

[1]Used by permission of The Woman's Press.

change. Instead of this Knight on a quest for the Holy Grail,

> "New light and new life—a new harmony yet
> To be run, and continued, and ended—"

instead of one who has in "the strong pain of pent knowledge . . . felt the new dawn,"[2] you have an exasperated young person a little sore at having the mood destroyed.

The young people cluster in the door of the chapel getting relights from those still in the protection of the church's walls. They gather around a single, shielded light on the campus and stay together that they may not be left alone in the dark. One boy gives it up as hopeless and, with an expression on his lips which was not quite in keeping with the words which he had heard in the chapel, throws down his candle and stomps disgustedly off to his room.

As we stood there on the chapel steps that night, Matthew Arnold's lines from "Rugby Chapel" came spontaneously to my lips:

> "What is the course of the life
> Of mortal men on the earth? . . .
> We, we have chosen our path—
> Path to a clear-purposed goal,
>   . . . but it leads
> A long steep journey, through sunk
> Gorges, o'er mountains of snow,
> Cheerful, with friends, we set forth—
> Then, on the height, comes the *wind*.

[2]Robert Browning, "Saul."

"Friends who set forth at our side,
Falter, are lost in the storm. . . .
Hardly ourselves we fought through,
Stripped, without friends, as we are. . . .
See! in the rocks of the world
Marches the host of mankind,
A feeble, wavering line.
Where are they tending? . . .
Ah, but the way is so long!
Years they have been in the wild! . . .
Factions divide them, their host
Threatens to break, to dissolve.
—Ah, keep, keep them combined!
Else of the myriads who fill
That army, not one shall arrive;
Sole they shall stray; in the rocks
Stagger for ever in vain,
Die one by one in the waste."

There on the windy campus was the lesson we had tried to teach them. It is not an easy world in which to be a Christian. To keep the light is not as simple as a word one says. Would they catch the urge in the final lines?

"Fill up the gaps in our files,
Strengthen the wavering line,
'Stablish, continue our march,
On, to the bound of the waste,
On, to the City of God."

I was grateful to the wind that night. It taught a lesson no words could convey, though we had told them:

"You go back to a windy world with only the candle flame of an individual desire to light its darkness. But a candle in the wind is not enough to light this world."

We must not let ourselves be fooled by the soft idea that this is just a different model of the same old world of men in which history, parrotlike, repeats itself; and therefore neither crises of depression nor victory's ecstasies should overly concern us.

There is, we know, a pattern in the way men live. It would be foolish to deny that. We can live with greater confidence because it is so. For no age can become so dark that it can blot out the memory that there did come a Renaissance. Yet neither should any Mount of Transfiguration make us forget the lunatic boy in the valley.

That history does repeat itself, although more in similarities than in exactness, saves us both from the pessimism of disappointed old age and the optimism of untested youth.

Said Gavin, The Little Minister of James Barrie, to Mr. Carfrae, his aged predecessor, as he bade the tired old man farewell:

"I begin where you leave off."

"Ah, Mr. Dishart," the white-haired minister said, with a sigh, "the world does not progress so quickly as a man grows old. You only begin where I began."

Neither was right, but of the two Mr. Carfrae the less right. For while life has a pattern, it does not stand still. Out of its repetitions there come things that are new and different—evil that never was and good that surpasses all before. When we call the current Public Enemy No. 1 a Jesse James, or war the modern expression of the Age of Chivalry, we are thinking loosely.

There are what biologists call emergents in the evolution of the world. When one passes out of one state of being into another, no unseen connection with a past can obscure a practical and evident difference —as different as is a mountain top from the valley at its foot.

One could do much with that analogy if one remembers that analogies must not be pushed too far. We are not trying to prove an exactness but, by piling up various impressions, to understand a difference.

I lay one summer's day at the foot of Mount Washington. The air was soft, the breeze gentle. The aroma of luxuriant vegetation, the drone of bees, the buzz of flies, made laziness in my bones. Life was easy and without time. But an object lay on my mind. There was a mountain to be scaled.

Reluctantly I threw my pack on my back and started up the Ammonoosuc Trail. In less than two hours I was in a different world. Scarcely perceptible was the change in latitude and longitude, but now the soft breeze had given way to a howling wind, the lazy air to gasping breath. Instead of fertile fields there were bare rocks, in place of foliage the stunted trees of the timber line. No longer relaxed, one's whole being braced against the tug and pull of rude nature.

There is a truth to be felt here. We cannot but see

—unless our eyes are wilfully blind—that the candle does not provide, in the world that is, a light adequate to let man see the world that must be.

Your life is a candle, so they told us in our youth. Be good yourself—"brighten the corner where you are." With such peaceful phrases our childhood was inspired.

We had the impression given *picturization* in another form by the Perry pictures of the "gentle Jesus, meek and mild," clad in a long white robe, strolling through flowery fields beside a placid lakeside, with a little lamb comfortably snuggled up in His arms and contented sheep looking up at Him from "green pastures" in which they had fed well.

Back to the candle analogy the Church came in its teaching and ornamented the moral by quoting to us the words of Portia, that good girl scout, who was coming back from having done her good deed for the day and sees the candle burning in her hallway. She says to her companion:

"How far that little candle throws his beams!
So shines a good deed in a naughty world."

It is not a naughty world—not in that indulgent sense, it is not. It is a desperately lost world. It is a world over which one must weep because it is as it is and we a part of it.

We are not in the Green Pastures; we are in the wilderness. Soörd makes the contrast in his great picture of "The Lost Sheep." We see the "desperate valley" with the overhanging mountains and the blackness of the imminent storm in the coming night. There on the ledge the lost sheep. Above him no soft-robed figure from a stained-glass window. A shepherd, weather-stained and strong, holds with one hand the jagged cliff and with the other reaches down to restore the lost.

We must make a similar contrast in our understanding of the place of religion in the modern world. It is not a new light we seek. The old light is the truth. But the candle is not enough. It won't do to be a good person in a sheltered spot. This age demands of those who believe in the truth of God, a light and a heat which cannot be blown out by the winds of the modern world. We must change our thinking about the Christian life as the "candle of the Lord" in two ways.

CHAPTER THREE

The Strength of Flame

HE torch is the symbol of those who care about the world. Candles are beautiful in homes, upon altars. They are adequate behind walls. But not outside. You must have at least a torch to move in the darkness of the wind and the road. Torches are the light for wayfarers.

A torch is more than a piece of wood. A piece of wood will burn. A torch has a special nature—it burns and is not consumed. It has the ability to drink up into itself and hold with spongelike eagerness the oil which bears the light through wind and rain.

". . . and is not consumed." That is not quite true. Even though saturated with oil it will at last become useless as a bearer of light. Carried in the night it may be lost and seem in the light of day a blackened stick thrown on some ash pile. Made brittle at last by constant heat, it may some day break and be cast aside.

But it will have carried the light for a time. Fill out the analogy as you see yourself living, moving, having your being in this world of men. The need of the world today is for men prodigal of themselves, saturated with the divine abandon. The self-conscious prodigality of burning a candle "at both ends" to make a "lovely light," is too weak to light our world. It is rather something of the urgency and the passion which we find in that line from Shelley, already mentioned. It is a light which "penetrates the frame of man's spirit" until he becomes "charged with the strength of flame."

The beginning of strength in religion is passion. Unless you feel, you will have little power to affect your world. One can, without passion, erect a life on this earth which is a monument to God, but a life which is a movement for God has to be greatly charged by burning feeling.

In trying to condense this curious feeling which Christianity produces—a feeling which hurts, and haunts, and is so strangely disordering to our lives, so often nicely arranged around moderate virtues— there was formed in my mind a description of what the Christ does to a man: *Christianity is a passion and a pilgrimage, a pulsing power, a breath-taking beauty, and a haunting memory of a past exaltation which may yet again return.*

This attempt to describe Christianity begins with the word *passion,* which has two meanings we should consider. The popular meaning needs to be looked at, lest we lose in its crudeness an important ingredient of religion. The other and more technically correct meaning of passion has a special significance for us, since without it Christianity has lost the vital spark which makes it important.

Passion means, first of all, intense feeling. This is dangerous, particularly because one may not have considered what caused the feeling and, stirred but not disciplined, one often moves stupidly and harmfully, or at least ineffectively.

Moses is a grand example of that. He is such a revealing friend to have by your side as you dwell in the startling extremes of the modern world, potentially one of the greatest civilizations man has yet known.

He had everything his way. Born of a race despised, persecuted, exploited, he was by the whim of Pharaoh's daughter brought up in the extremes of privilege. As he rode his chariot through the Harlem of his city to the playing fields to the north on the green banks of the Nile, he was dimly conscious of these people of his own race who were somehow not living in very happy surroundings.

At the Club he had talked it over with Amenhotep, wealthy young member of the ruling class, but had met a frosty stare and comment, "Stop talking like a Communist." Moses shrugged his shoulders and ended his momentary concern with the comment, "Oh, well, it's a pretty good world after all."

But the question did not quite vanish from his mind. Every once in a while it popped up again disturbingly. "After all," he thought, "it is not quite right to have this slum area there almost at our doors." He took to wandering down into the back parts of the city and he felt more and more uncomfortable.

Then one day he saw a husky foreman beating up a poor bewildered workman who had made a complaint about working conditions (something about a "stretch-out" and "bricks without straw"). Suddenly Moses saw red. Feeling blazed into a passion. He struck the Egyptian and knocked him down. Still flaming with passion, he waited for the foreman to rise. Then in horror he stooped. The man was dead. Passion oozed out of him. Fear came in.

As a Negro who had struck a white man in the South would run, so Moses fled from the result of his passion.

Obviously passion—uncontrolled, undisciplined—had made matters worse rather than better. I imagine that conditions for the Israelites in the brickyards of Pharaoh were not improved that day the dead body of the Egyptian foreman was found lying in the street outside the gate.

Imagine? One knows. Walk the streets of some Southern city in the days following a blow struck— even though in defense of the right to his own home— by some Negro. The Israelites walked softly and in terror for weeks following Moses' passionate act.

There is much of young Moses in the world today and so-called wise heads shake dolefully about it. "Just see," they say, "how destructive your senti-mental ideas are."

Moreover, passion, in the popular sense of the word, is often a twisted concern. What better examples could one have than Saul of Tarsus "breathing out threatenings and slaughter" against the early Chris-tians, or the members of the Inquisition who were so passionately concerned about men's beliefs that they tortured unorthodox believers horribly to make them recant heresy and accept the faith?

What greater folly could passion—uncontrolled, undisciplined—show than the history of the Crusades and particularly that ill-fated Children's Crusade of 1212 where, without anything but an idea, thousands of children from all over Germany and France followed the pipe of passion? As the rats and mice—and the children—went after the Pied Piper out of Hamelin, so these children imitated the acts of their elders until, stranded far from home, most of them became slaves, as their passion spent itself and their meager preparations for their crusade failed.

Yes, passion takes curious quirks. It can be very destructive of good values as it "roots out and pulls down and destroys." There is reason for good men as well as bad to fear the passion which explodes.

Yet even taking it on its worst side let us think for a moment how much worse life would be without it. When Dante pictured the lowest depths of hell it was not fire but ice which encompassed the souls of men. The poor sinners could not even weep because their first tears froze and formed a block of ice to shut out vision and congeal further tears. "I did not weep," one says, "I was so turned to stone within."

A queer thought entered my brain one day and naturally was at first rejected. My mind said, "It is not so." But the idea persisted and would not let me rest and now seems to me to be a part of the Mind of God.

*I believe God would rather have us want something
wrong than to have us not want anything at all.* God
is frustrate because we have no passion. He can bring
a prodigal home redeemed from the far country, but
the lethargic self-fullness of the elder brother is a
barrier in the path of God.

You must *want* a better world before you have any
chance of getting it. Christianity must become a passion—a controlled passion if possible, a disciplined
passion if one can—but a passion, if it is to be effective.

The ground for hope in the Church today is not
that we have seen through to the end with wisdom
but that, believing there is an end, we are determined
to seek and find it.

Passion even in the popular and often destructive
sense is in the Church today as reason for hope and
is the promise of attainment. God would rather have
us want something wrong than have us not want anything at all.

Passion, however, really means something far different from the popular sense in which we have just
used it. It it not only an errant feeling, a wild urgency
to do something because obviously something needs
to be done. It is not only an emotional drive which in
times of blindness sets us reaching for the nearest
pillar to pull the temple down over the heads of the
people. It is a sensitiveness—a capability. It is the
capacity of being affected.

In this sense passion means: do you have by nature,
or have you gained by experience; and have you developed in your nature and retained in spite of some

experiences, a sensitiveness to beauty (and to ugliness) so that you stretch constantly toward the beauty and are forever discontent with ugliness?

Have you the capacity for being strongly affected—deeply, hauntingly hurt—by those areas in our common life which by their very existence in that life make constant and embarrassing denial of the truth we profess? Does your idea of Christianity keep you caring—sleeplessly at times, unceasingly within the limits of your powers—about men out of work, and child labor, and our stupid national self-importance which periodically sends out the best we have to tear at each other with the blind passion of dogs in a street fight? How do you feel when you see all the ingenuity of our keenest minds used to throw the whole next generation out at last physically, mentally, and spiritually—but scraps of useless refuse on the dung heap of a lunatic world?

Jesus said, Blessed are they that mourn—who have the capacity for caring deeply—for they shall be comforted. Yes, and they shall be the comfort of—they shall bring comfort at last to—the world.

"Comfort ye, comfort ye my people," said Isaiah, and right under it were the words, "The voice of him that crieth in the wilderness, Prepare ye the way of the Lord, make straight in the desert a highway for our God." Here is where you begin to test yourself to find out whether the passion of Christ's spirit is in you.

Is war upon the face of the earth? What do you feel? Do you say, "Oh that's the inevitable result of human nature, as impossible to prevent as to keep flies from buzzing about a bit of carrion in the summer heat"?

Does race run riot in the streets of our great cities: does a colored man chained to a tree try to gulp in the flame which is his only mercy then as it snuffs out his life while a grim mob exultingly hisses over his sizzling flesh? How about your blood then? Does it remain cool in your head as you think, "Oh they are only white ants and black contending over their hills of dust"?

Do classes engaged in industrial conflicts and in that class warfare—however necessary some passionate followers of the Christ may claim it to be—nevertheless make fundamental denial of their professed faith. What think you of it? Spiders and bugs struggling for supremacy in cobwebs in the corners of tumble-down buildings?

Do you remember the first time you realized that men, women, and little children were caught in the relentless grinding of a machine-like industrial system which had power beyond anything we have ever known before to take from the backs of humanity the burden of poverty? Yet that world was afraid of losing the privileges of the few, and so created an artificial scarcity in the midst of plenty to sustain or recover a false prosperity. Have you become so used to a policy of "better not touch" that you say, "Oh well, that's the way of the world"; or are you still searching, with a hurting sense of your own sin, to discover the processes by which our power may become the door of opportunity to the abundant life for every one?

Here is passion pressing, beating at your consciousness. As you read these uncomfortable, these disordering words, do you feel as one fine-grained woman confessed to me one day she did. "You spoke of the New Earth of our profession of faith which demanded a willingness, an eager gladness, in accepting the fact of change. I sat there," she told me, "resisting the implications of what you said with every fiber of my being." Are you, in her spirit, crying, "O let me rest"? Or do you want the cleavage to be clearly marked between the worldly standards and the gospel of the Christ?

Religion at its best is conscience in action. Christianity is the best in religion as we conceive it, and because of our profession more is demanded of us. A convinced Buddhist may not have the compulsion to feel as we feel. A Confucianist with all the beauty of thought and calmness of action of that high religion is not expected to care as we care. But Christ did care. It hurt Him that men stood idle in the market place because no man would hire them; that men were possessed of devils which divided them; that privileged groups, scribes and pharisees, were so blind to their opportunities and responsibilities, neither going in to possess the promised land of the spirit incarnate in the Kingdom of God on earth, nor allowing those who desired it thirstily to go in.

We know as we look on Him that His passion was bigger than the time He had and the body in which

He dwelt. An infinite love confined in the limitation of flesh bursts the bonds of control at times and fiercely cries out with intense and uncontrolled passion, Woe! Woe! Woe! One cannot always speak with discretion in such a world as His—or ours. His passion, both in the senses of intense feeling and of capacity for caring—capability of being affected—killed Him. It was not the scribes and pharisees—those corporate interests concerned for their interests. They were what they were and better men than they have knuckled under to them before this. But they were only the environment of His existence.

His passion killed Him. There was that within Him which could not rest in such a world. Because He cared so much He died when He did. Procula, the wife of Pilate, recognized that fact—that He was responsible for His own death—when in Masefield's play, "Good Friday," she tells her dream of one poor man's naked intelligence pitted against the world and being crushed. She says sadly, and yet touched with a sense of its glory, that He was not blind. It was only that "the lonely exaltation of His mind" made Him hungry and athirst and because of that He was The Unafraid. She goes on to say that it is only the unafraid in life's roaring street who do touch beauty's feet, know truth, and become God's son.

A man comes at times to the place at which he can face the knowledge that his chances of seeing the consummation of his hopes are small. He may know that well. But this, too, he knows: that only the unafraid catch the passion of a spirit which calls to us, today as then, to rest not nor to be weary, because we are resiliently determined to live "life in scorn of consequences" until the Kingdom comes. Christ's way waits for passion to bear fruit in the lives of men. Men will know Christ only as they see in us the unconquerable passion for perfection which was the daring joy He gave to the world.

"I beseech you therefore, brethren, that ye present yourselves, holy, acceptable unto God, which is your reasonable service." The world needs men in whom the passion of Christ's spirit is not missing.

CHAPTER FOUR

The Things We Accept

BEFORE we add the third conception of the light to the idea of the candle and the torch, we should be sure we see the contrast between the spirit of Christ's passion and our own way of looking at the world. Our passion for the right so often lacks the power of sustained indignation and passes all too easily into taking some evil in the world as one of the things we must accept.

We are not yet through with Moses. Again he makes us "see ourselves as others see us," as in the hills of Midian he forgets the ills of Egypt. The voice of God spoke disturbingly to him there in one of the great calls to the conscience of man. Let's give that scene a modern setting.

A boy stood in the rain outside a world-famous church in Birmingham, England, one summer night. John Henry Jowett of Fifth Avenue was returning to his old pulpit at Carr's Lane to preach on that Sunday. A line of people waited for the doors to open. The only thing the boy remembers is a text which was the spark that set Moses going, and Moses was one of his heroes.

I stood in the pulpit of the Congregational Church

of Birmingham, Alabama, one day and there before me was the pulpit Bible of John Henry Jowett sent to the church in Birmingham, Alabama, as an encouragement to the church in new Birmingham from the church in Birmingham, England. I opened the Bible of John Henry Jowett and read the text from which he preached that day.

"I have seen, I have seen the affliction of my people which is in Egypt, and I have heard their groaning by reason of their taskmasters and am come down to deliver them. And now come, I will send thee into Egypt."

I have always found it difficult to preach upon that text. It is so much greater in itself, it is so much fuller in its association, than my capacity to express.

The Old Testament gives us insight for our daily lives. It mirrors man. The New Testament is equally honest—neither Testament is at all afraid of truth. They reveal man as he is; they paint life "with the warts on." But the New Testament glows with an almost unearthly light. In it are set down life's radiant moments when men suddenly become different—at least while Jesus is there. Transcending the common day, it is not easy to calm its disturbing effect on the feelings.

The disordering experience of knowing the Peace of God is shown by Tennyson in his "King Arthur" where he says:

> "his work . . . being done,
> Let visions of the night or of the day
> Come as they will; . . .

Until this earth he walks on seems not earth,
This light that strikes his eyeball is not light,
This air that smites his forehead is not air
But vision—"

This is a moment when he "feels he cannot die." That is why Peter tried to walk on water and why the disciples thought they could cast out devils. The New Testament is sane with the sanity of God, which nearly drives men mad.

The Old Testament is nearer to man's earthly experience. Forty years' wandering in the wilderness is a more natural process of achieving the promised land than the New Testament's "this day is salvation come into thy house." And it is in the Old Testament that we see ourselves as we are more naturally.

Moses, who is so like us, is again our help. He accepted things. That story-book life has already been sketched. We limn it again quickly for our special accent. Born a Jew, when to be born a Jew meant death on the swords of Pharaoh's soldiers, he was saved by a strange combination of circumstances and brought up by Pharaoh's daughter. Everything which money and power could bring he had. His body grew strong and skillful instead of getting rickets in the slums. His mind, fed on the culture of ages, was made keen by the contact with the best minds of the court, instead of picking up its knowledge from the street and being sharpened only by the struggle to exist. Boundless his opportunity as wish could claim instead of limited by a dead-end alley. Favored child of fortune; pampered of the gods. As one boy remarked one day on hearing his story, "He got the breaks."

He accepted them, as you and I. It was not without conscience. The playing fields on the outskirts of the city were not as care-free that day on which the riot in the Jewish quarter was put down sternly by the soldiers of Pharaoh. Moses sent in a subscription that night to the Society for the Advancement of the Jewish people, though he had heard at the Club that they were touched with radicalism. Yet all the while he accepted things—this rising young favorite of the court.

It is possible he might have continued on his conventional way had he not seen with his own eyes a foreman beat a Jewish brickmaker. His pent-up dissatisfaction with such conditions boiled over and he stepped in between them and knocked the foreman down. We have already seen the error in that type of passion. We did not mark, when we looked at the story first, how quickly thought of self came in to wipe out his passion for the right.

Frightened, Moses fled. Would a Jew flee in Germany who had struck a Nazi? Would a Negro flee in—oh, let's not put it in the South, Harlem will do. Would a Negro flee in Harlem for knifing a manager of a store, let's say? Moses fled. Favorite though he was, he was a *Jewish* favorite and he did not feel safe until the far-off hills of Midian were beneath his feet.

There, making good, he married a wife; was heir apparent to the best sheep business in the country;

and forgot the slums of Egypt. He accepted things again. Even as you and I.

But to the sensitive heart the voice of God is always speaking. The haunting memory of a people's bondage would not let him rest. And one day he heard the voice of God more clearly than you can hear a man speak because you can listen with your ears and short-circuit truth from one ear to the other. The voice he heard was still and small but was within. No noise could drown it, no speed escape it.

"Moses, what about my people—your people and mine? 'I have seen, I have seen the affliction of my people which is in Egypt and I have heard their groaning (because of their taskmasters) and am come down to deliver them. And now come, I will send thee into Egypt.'"

"Listen, Lord," the man who accepted things said in agony, "you know that it is dangerous for me to go back there. I killed a man once. I didn't mean to. I was defending a brother from abuse—but they won't consider that. Besides, what can I do? I have no power against the principalities and powers of Egypt. Send Aaron. He is smooth of tongue. He can argue this matter with Pharaoh."

The voice of God replied: "I have seen, I have seen the affliction of my people which is in Egypt and I have heard their groaning because of their taskmasters and I have come down to deliver them. And now come, I am sending thee into Egypt."

"But, God of my fathers, I cannot go now. This is

the busy season in the sheep business. My lambs need shearing. My fences need repairing. After all, conditions in the brick business in Egypt have been bad a long time. The wise men have truly said, 'The poor ye have always with you.' "

Thus Moses argued with the voice of God which spoke in human need.

The voice of God replied: "I have seen, I have seen the affliction of my people which is in Egypt and I have heard their groaning because of their taskmasters and I have come down to deliver them. And now come, I am sending thee into Egypt."

And Moses went. The voice would not let him accept things. How tragic it would have been if he had not followed his call! Suppose he had left to other leadership the exodus from Egypt. If in the wilderness, discouraged, the people should have had only some Aaron with smooth tongue in cheek to turn to as their highest authority, some Aaron who would weakly have let them bow down before a golden calf forever, what would the history of mankind have been?

With this scene as background, with the sense of Moses in the great cloud of witnesses to our ways now, let's think about the things we know. What do you know that you card-catalogue in the neat compartments of your mind and accept as knowledge without responsibility?

We know that brotherhood is an idle word when men have made of many bloods the common race of man to be scattered confusedly on the face of the earth. The Jew is outcast. Unconquered but defeated he walks buffeted and beaten through the passages of time. "Isn't that just like a Jew?" we say, when some disagreeably pushing person crosses our path. "Which Jew do you mean, Shylock or Christ?" we might ask, but it shakes us only for a moment. We accept as an inevitable our dislike of an attitude, not the sole possession of the Jew, although by our common action so often forced upon him; and we isolate a race.

We accept the fact that the Jew is outcast. Feebly we make a gesture on brotherhood day, which comes but once a year.

We know that millions of our fellow-citizens suffer because of the color of their skins. The old Sunday School hymn comes liltingly to mind,

"The little black baby who rolls in the sand,
 In the land far over the sea,
 Is my African brother and Jesus loves him
 Just as He loves you and me."

Little black children look cute in mission magazines but you ought to have seen the trouble involved in entering one in a school which curiously bore the name of the great emancipator of the black race.

We accept Harlem and all it implies. "Yes, we do," you say, "but what can we do about it? I have no power. Besides, Negroes in my section would hurt business values. This is not a problem we can handle. Isn't that reasonable? What do you say to that?" I said, "There are things we accept."

These illustrations are obvious and obviously are proper for examples of one of the hardest facts of our religion. My church has stood for one hundred years on Broadway and now is proclaiming the worship of God-the-Father, in a section of the city where the infant death rate is nearly twice the average for the city. It is one of the worst sections for tuberculosis because people have not enough light, and air, and food. One of our members who sat recently on the criminal side of the Grand Jury reports that the recurrence of addresses in the West 50's and 60's became almost a horror, there were so many. The church stands on one of the edges of old Hell's Kitchen, which still cooks up its stews. Not a pleasant thought that we worship where the city's scums make fevered and fetid the spiritual air we breathe.

Do not feel that life is all mud and misery. Men are glorious and life has its heroic moments. This is not a dark and dismal existence. There is joy and power and a sense of beauty.

But we who know *that* have an obligation. We cannot rest on our hills of Midian content. We must not accept things which deny the religion we profess. We must care about what is and what is not, and when we care enough things change. It is the way the world works. It is the haunted souls who save the world. And when you feel, as some of you do, the unreconciled spirit of the God we see in Christ, we shall together take up our responsibility so that brotherhood—disordering as it is to our simple peace

—will be neither an idol nor an idle word. Not to accept things is the mark of the Christian in an un-
brotherly world.

On the back of an envelope I had scrawled one day
an arresting description by E. A. Robinson of Matthias, the successful man who was absorbed in good
deeds without creating good: "He was in harmony
even with chaos." And Garth, though himself un-
successful, did know what was wrong with Matthias
as he said, "You are not sound in your serenity."

Lying in an upper berth, I was haunted by that
description and thought on *The Peace of God*. Beneath the lines of Robinson I found these words pour-
ing from my pencil as the train roared through the
night:

I

A man went up into the church,
   As his custom was,
   And bowed his head.
He closed his eyes
   And prayed for the Peace of God:
   "Pax Dei Mecum.
Send down Thy light."

When he opened his eyes he could see
   Nothing, for a moment.
The light was brighter
   Than he had ever known it
   And made all things seem not solid.
The walls of the church were no longer there,
   (Or so he thought).

When his eyes became accustomed to the light
He saw:
    Two million men, women, and children
    Jammed into a few square miles of filthy tene-
        ments;
    Beaten men standing in bread lines in the rain;
    Prison cells crowded with empty lives.

He cried out sharply,
    "How long have *you* been there?"
In a mutter of dull voices the answer rose:
    "Always!"

He shut his eyes and said,
    "O God; I cannot bear this sight!"

A Voice replied,
    "But you asked for the Peace of God:
    To see is a portion of My Peace."

II

He moved his lips
    And prayed for the Peace of God:
    "Pax Dei Mecum.
    Speak, Lord, Thy servant heareth."

With closed eyes (that he might not see)
    He waited for a silence
    To still the confusion of sounds.

No silence came,
    But the sound lost its cacophony.

A low murmur came closer
And he realized the march of many feet.
A command rang out, "Halt!
Go, roam the world without a place to rest.
They need our graves to cradle babies
Unborn when last we fought.
Break ranks!"

The confusion of sound began again
And underneath it all
The shuffle of ghostly feet.

Over his ears he cupped his hands,
"O God! I cannot bear this sound!"

A Voice replied:
"But you asked for the Peace of God:
To hear is a portion of My Peace."

III

He raised his hands
And prayed for the Peace of God:
"Pax Dei Mecum.
Who is sufficient for these things?"

(There came the sound of many voices:)

"I heard Thy Voice . . . and was afraid."
"Am I my brother's keeper?"
"I am but a child; I cannot speak."
"Woe is me . . . I am unclean."
"This thing is too heavy for *me*—
    I am not able to perform it."

"I, even I alone, am left."
"I am not worthy to be called Thy son."
   (Make me as one of Thy servants
   Who works by the day for wages.)

A Voice replied:
   "But you asked for the Peace of God:
     'To have no rest in your spirit
       Because you found not your brother';
     'To remember them that are in bonds,'
       And to be not free when any 'suffer
         adversity';
     'To feel the obligations of a friend'
       When you take the name of My Son,
         Jesus:

"This is a portion of My Peace.
   Go forth in Peace.
   Pax Dei Tecum."

L'ENVOI

The man arose.
The walls of the church,
   Though there, were not the same.
     His step was firm.
     His eyes were bright.
     His head was high.
     His voice rang clear:
"Here am I, send me!"

   To see, to hear, to feel,
"To work the work of Him that sent me."
   This, now, is my peace,

"For my heart is restless until it rests
  In Thee."

"I can do all things through Christ
  Who strengtheneth me."

CHAPTER FIVE

Life Needs a Cutting Edge

*I*T IS not enough to possess a truth which, burning on some protected altar, can soothe the soul with thoughts that:

"God, by God's own ways occult,
May—doth, I will believe—bring back
All wanderers to a single track.
Meantime, I can but testify
God's care for me—"[1]

Nor is it enough to proclaim that truth, cost what it may. We hear William Lloyd Garrison as he speaks about the evil of slavery which good people were accepting as inevitable:

"I will be as harsh as truth, and as uncompromising as justice. On this subject I do not wish to think, or speak, or write with moderation. I am in earnest—I will not equivocate—I will not excuse—I will not retreat a single inch—and I will be heard."

Thrilling as those words are, do not forget another William, named Wilberforce, who faced the less dramatic but in some ways more terrible slavery in the

[1]Robert Browning, "Christmas Eve."

British Empire. Read the story of that man, at first not wanting to see, who could not rest at last until the evil of human slavery was wiped out in the Empire. It is only after one hundred years that its drama is evident to all. There was dullness in the doing of it.

It is more fun to be a Garrison. It is easier in its way. To be dragged about Boston Common with a rope around one's waist, while derisive voices anticipate the sickening thud of a stone on human flesh, has an age-old ecstasy to it which martyrs have always known. There is a peace to being helpless in the hands of persecutors—a feeling that now your cause is in the hands of God.

To be still yourself a hand for God, responsible to Him for that hand's skill . . . To have to hold on with the patience of God through years when men would not see at first and having seen would not do . . . To be near victory at the beginning when men voted "Aye" as a sentimentalism, but when they saw that the idea might win and that it would cost them much, changed to a "practical" man's "Nay" . . . To work for eighteen years and be farther from the goal than when you began . . . To be wasted in health, restless, unhappy, frustrate, and yet knowing you must go on . . . All this tests the stuff of a man.

That Wilberforce won in twenty years and slavery officially was no more in the British Empire makes him one of the fortunate adventurers for God. Most men do not find such a twenty-year-long short-cut to a goal. The lifetime of a man is not ordinarily long enough to make an acorn-idea become the prac-

tical oak. One dwells in the fairyland of Jack's Bean-
stalk, if he does not know that the seeker after God's
truth must not be motivated by the reward of victory.
Man must walk a lonely road and often die with no
actual proof of the worth of having walked it, because
he is realistic enough to know that in ultimate truth
is man's only hope.

But Wilberforce is valuable to us not so much because he won as for the way in which he won. To an
idea and to a feeling he added efficacy—realistic, per-
sistent, unweariable.

It is at this point that Christianity has failed so
often. The most important thing to notice about the
age-old problems of the world is not that man has
not ideals enough nor that there are not men who will
proclaim these ideals fearlessly. It is that no considerable group of mankind holds to the ideal as its
supreme motivation and brings to bear on the life
we live an intelligent and effectual movement toward
the goal.

In Revelation there is a condemnation of one of
the early churches in words we may thus rightly ex-
pand: "You have a glorious heritage, a great tradition,
and a reputation of being a church of real significance;
but I have found nothing which you have done which
is complete in the eyes of God."

This fact does not trouble us as it should. Those of
us who have any conscience at all think more or less,
now and then, about the gap between what we know
and what we do. We are even conscious that there
are some things of which we might easily become

aware, if only we did not think it wiser to be ignorant. At the moment we can just mention for purposes of illustration two things we know.

We know that race is a festering sore. Conscious and unconscious, bitter and complacent barriers are erected between man and man and between men and women because of the colors of skin and the shape of features. A black man passing down the street of white houses gives voice to the hopelessness of his race's exclusion:

> "Your door is shut against my tightened face,
> And I am sharp as steel with discontent;
> But I possess the courage and the grace
> To bear my anger proudly and unbent.
>
> .   .   .   .
>
> Oh I must search for wisdom every hour,
> Deep in my wrathful bosom sore and raw,
> And find in it the superhuman power
> To hold me to the letter of your law!
> Oh I must keep my heart inviolate
> Against the potent poison of your hate."[2]

This is one of the things we know: That our Christianity is damned daily by the lack of success in changing such a situation.

We know that industry has a tendency to go to sleep on the side of human relationships. Industry made a success of producing efficiently great quantities of goods. This is good. But even as a man, concentrating so hard on a problem that his foot goes to

[2]Claude McKay, "White Houses," in *Survey Graphic*, March, 1925.

sleep, finds himself unable to walk on a leg over which he seems to have no control and which has a feeling of separation from his body, so we find ourselves today facing what many feel to be an inevitable conflict of class with class because we did not make a success of human relationships.

This does not mean there is fear of revolution, which is still distant from immediate concern. But, as Christian people, it should concern us greatly that our major emphasis is not to be a *laissez-faire* attitude of let bad enough alone. We are not here to preserve a system. We are set to produce some way of living together which will make successful, in the realm of humanity, the principle of brotherhood which we profess. No organization of society which does not succeed in that deserves the support of any who bear the name of Christ. This is a fact almost too obvious to mention. This is one of the things we know and in which we must succeed if we are to make effective the Christianity we profess.

To be conscious of this gap between what we know and what we do is to demand that the light we hold to be the truth be organized in such a way that it shall be not only worshipped and proclaimed but effective in removing evil and constructing good. The modern organization of light in the acetylene torch is the obvious picture symbol. This is the next step in man's use of the responsibility of light.

There must come into the process of living such a manner of handling the light that it shall have the power of the acetylene torch to cut through existing

obstacles in the way of progress with all the apparent
ease of a hot knife through butter. There must be
added also that quality by which it is possible to lay
cold steel end to end and, by the organization of the
light, fuse those separate pieces into one strong and
effective structure: to bridge streams, to hold up
buildings, and to conquer the impossible.

We may be well-intentioned and our ideals may be
beautiful and good. We may be unafraid to speak the
truth we know and sincere in our desire for the
victory of truth. Obviously, however, we are not
intelligent unless we have on hand and know how to
use effective tools. The Christian life needs its instruments of precision, keen-edged, well-tempered tools
of "word, thought, and deed" if it is to develop a
strategy, to construct a way, to transform the world.
Christianity needs to be in our minds and work in our
lives with a cutting edge.

This is what Jesus meant by the statement, "I came
not to send peace, but a sword." This often misapplied
text is easily misunderstood, but even a pure literalist
has to put on narrow blinders to make it out as an
argument for going to war.

Jesus as usual was talking about thinking rather
than about things. As Isaiah had you and me in mind
instead of lions and calves in his famous prophecy
about "a little child shall lead them"; so Jesus was
speaking here about a spiritual attitude, not a physical
action.

"Even as"—our more prosaic minds might need to
have it explained as so often the disciples had to ask

what the parables meant—"Even as a war situation
often splits families (look at our Civil War), separates
friends, cuts across other loyalties, so is the gospel,"
Jesus is saying. "I did not come to soothe you with
soft words; to 'cry peace, peace, when there is no
peace'; to let you rest content in your past goodness.
I came to call for a choice as straightly fixed as are
your decisions when a nation goes to war. It will set
father against son, mother against daughter, if need
be. I came to have you see that there is truth and
falsehood; that good enough is bad when 'be ye perfect even as your father in heaven is perfect' is your
goal. Across your 'ancient good' will be marked 'un-
couth' if you think that the honorable good of old
is enough for 'the present crisis.' 'He that is not with
me is against me.' 'I came not to send peace, but a
sword.' " Read in its context it is evident that Jesus
was talking about the divisive character of the truth.

It is a characteristic of good that it becomes contented with itself. One of the startling effects of Jesus
upon men was that the cleavage was made clear between the good and the perfect. In the light of that
keen-edged mind we become aware that most of us
are not good workmen with our tools. We botch too
much of the material of life because we have no skill.

It is a valuable spiritual experience every once in a
while to watch a skillful surgeon perform an operation. We can learn much from the sight of those sure
hands, that purposeful procedure. There is an order
to an operation which is very stimulating. Each movement follows rightly the one preceding. It is "begun,

continued, and ended," to use the words of the old prayer, "and once begun it must be finished."

How much of possible value is buried in spiritual graveyards under the dull clods of our sentimental good intentions because we neither rightly diagnosed nor skillfully excised the evil growth imbedded there. We need to learn to handle our tools.

This means that there must be in our perception and presentation of the truth of Christianity an exactness of understanding and a sharpness of action that cut. This is the supreme loyalty—to let the knife-edge of truth fall where it should, cost what it may. If we are true to Christ's vision of man we must keep in our minds the idea of the perfect life.

Does that really mean perfect? Yes, it means perfect.

Why not? Why should we who profess Christ's way stop always with the cross of failure? We almost glory in it. We do glory in it. We should be disappointed *if* we did not have failure to prove how glorious is our faith. We have our minds adjusted to failure. It justifies the largeness of our claims about the infinite truth of Christianity.

We put a false valuation on the Christian life when we say that it is a rare and difficult achievement.

But if just anybody can do it—the butcher, the baker, the candlestick maker, can butch, and bake, and electric bulbs make, and be perfect too—well . . .

We stop the sentence in mid-air. Our ideas have no landing place. We had sort of assumed that the struggle to attain was sufficient justification for existence and that the supreme failure would be to reach the goal and have nothing left for which to struggle.

But He never preached that. He said we were to be perfect even as God is perfect. One of His great interpreters described the perfect life of word, thought and deed, which Jesus demanded, as the "reasonable" life.

And the point is that it does not seem so unreasonable, after all, if you do go after it as a scientist searches for an answer or as an engineer builds a bridge. "Begun, continued, and ended," from the known to the unknown continually.

There are certain things in which you are perfect now. You would not rob a crying baby of its crust of bread. I begin very low. You would give up your life for your friend. That seems like a big jump? But there are no jumps in the perfect. Not stealing the baby's crust and unreservedly letting your lifeblood flow out for a friend are in their own narrow ways perfect. The imperfection is outside them in snatching your own security from babies whom you never see, or letting men die—men who might have been saved by your life, although you have not known they might be friends. But the idea of an effective Christian life affirms it is not impossible to widen the circle of your intimate concern and, in areas where it does not now operate, to live perfectly there too, even as you now do perfectly in some narrower circles of your own personal concerns.

Let me point this up by describing a cartoon which has been haunting and helpful ever since I first saw it.

It is a very simple picture which was in one of the
Christmas numbers of *Punch*. A caption of only two
sentences describes it.

Before I describe it, there is another picture I want
you to see. The figure of a girl is in my mind. She
is one of the witnesses during the Relief Investigation
some of us held one winter. She is about twenty-one
and has herself and a little baby to support in this,
"Our Father's," world. She had had a husband but
he had lost his job and then lost his nerve and had
run away. We need mention no names, you see. The
story is without number and without date.

We asked her what she did and discovered that she
sewed buttons and little adornments on dresses to
make them practical and pretty for our wives and
daughters to wear—dresses that sold for $1.95. I had
not realized that dresses could be made for that.

"How much have you made this week?" (It was
Wednesday then.)

"Seventy cents," she said.

"What! A day?"

"No, for the last two days."

Working ten hours a day to do it! Paid by the
dress, and so many extra gadgets on each dress that
she made no more than that. This is not unusual. You
know that.

She worked twenty hours and she was paid seventy
cents to keep herself and a little baby alive in Our
Father's world.

We drove them out of New York and they went
up into Connecticut, those firms that are well called

sweatshops. Connecticut drove them out, and they went over into New Jersey. New Jersey became excited about them for a moment, as we all did, but maybe they forgot again, too. They are somewhere now—those sweatshops. Some of them came back to New York, because I found one during Christmas week almost within the shadow of the tower of my church.

One of my fine young women made an interesting remark about this type of thing the other day. "A dress at $1.95 used to be for me a good value," she said. "Now it has become a problem in values."

With that personification of the problem of values sitting before you, let's look at the cartoon.

In a high-backed armchair before a big fireplace in which a fire burns cheerfully, sits a little old lady. She is a good little old lady. I speak with no derision. She has done many good things. It is Christmas Eve. She has sent her regular Christmas baskets to the poor of the parish. She has told the minister, as she does regularly, that if there are any special needs to be sure and call upon her. She has treated her servants well and remembered her friends. She is good, even as you and I.

Now she is ready to have the house closed for the night. She has given her last orders to the butler who stands respectfully before her. She thinks of one more thing, and this is what the line beneath the picture says:

"Pearson, since it is Christmas Eve, don't use the

regular cheese tonight. Put some of our best Stilton in the mousetraps this evening."

I shall never be able to think of the work of the Church without question again. We do many good works, but the truly Christian life demands that we do not fool ourselves into thinking that to occupy our time in good works is sufficient justification for our existence.

The world has not changed in its need nor in the truth which is its solution. We need light. But a candle in the wind is not enough for this world's need.

CHAPTER SIX

Sources of Power as Jesus Found Them

HE most difficult question in the spiritual life is—HOW? It needs to be asked. It needs to be answered as well as one can. But it is not easy. The disciples saw Jesus cast a devil out of a man with whom they had worked and failed. "Why could not we cast him out?" was the way in which they phrased the old question, "*How* did you do that?"

Jesus told them—but even after they knew they did not know. We are often up against the honest doubt of Nicodemus—"How *can* a man be born again?" But sometimes we feel the winds of the spirit blow and know that we cannot longer be what we were, and now we ask, "*How* can a man be born again?"

The change in accent from doubt to desire is the beginning of knowledge, but it is only within that we know something has happened. "This kind," said Jesus, "comes out only with prayer and fasting."

"Yes, but we prayed about it too," Christians have said from that day to this. "The fact is we did everything you did and it did not happen—this release of a man from bondage to evil. *How* did you do it?"

There is a story, which is to the point, about a musical prodigy who was given an audition by a great musician. The child had a touch of genius and the great artist, recognizing it, said some encouraging words. Flushed with the praise, the child released from his sense of reserve a deep-down longing. "Oh, Master," he said, "I want to compose too. Tell me, how do you compose?"

The master looked with kindly eye on the child and said gently, "Live, wait, listen, learn, feel, some day you will compose."

"But," said the infant prodigy, "you composed when you were seven."

"Yes," said the master. "It is true that I composed when I was seven. But I did not have to ask anybody how."

This does not mean there are not things which can be taught and can be learned, else is all experience ultimately in vain since each must then learn always by the hard way of experience instead of the sane way of a disciplined imagination. But let no one think that the how of spiritual power is a matter of definition or technique. You can teach people the motions but not the emotions of life. You can mold man into the model of perfection; it is not so easy to breathe into the form the breath of life so that he lives and acts like a man.

As we come to the place where we are to think more exactly about how to make the light we hold effective in the world we live in, we are faced with a momentary quandary. Shall we begin logically with our ideas of God—and if man would begin there he would make fewer mistakes—or shall we move as most men do, from himself and his world to the idea and the Presence of God? Chronologically in the experience of most men the next chapter should precede, not follow, this one.

We can make this dilemma only a hesitation by centering our problem of dynamics in the person of Jesus, and asking ourselves the question, "What Were the Sources of Power as Jesus Found Them?" Something made *Him* go. What was it? Why did He do what He did? How did He get His power?

Beyond that, how did He expect us to live and move and have our being so that we would get that power too?

There is not the slightest question that He did expect us to get power. "The things I do ye shall do and greater things than these shall ye do." "You cannot follow me now, but you will follow me afterwards." "To as many as *believed*, to them gave he **power to become** the sons and daughters of God."

Uttered and unexpressed the record is clear. He expected us to do what He said. We are going to ask ourselves therefore the question, What are the sources of power as Jesus found them? And how do we find that power too?

It is obvious that we begin with Jesus' consciousness of God. His life with God was the fundamental reality. "I must be about My Father's business." "I and the Father are one." "He that hath seen Me hath seen the Father." "O righteous Father, the world

hath not known Thee but I have known Thee and
these have known that Thou hast sent Me. And I
have declared unto them Thy name, and I will de-
clare it, that the love wherewith Thou hast loved
Me may be in them and I in them."

These are typical and constant expressions of Jesus'
feeling. His whole teaching about the Kingdom was
rooted and grounded in the sure sense of life with
God.

Moreover, while by isolating out of their contexts
some of Jesus' comments about His own ministry you
could make it appear that Jesus was holding up His
own place of importance in the idea of things, yet
when you see the total effect of Jesus' witness it was
immovably God-centered. "Why callest Thou *Me*
good, there is none good save *God*." "Let your light
so shine before men that they may see your good
works and glorify *God*." "Not as I will but as Thou
wilt." His life was centered in God. And that life
with God gave Him power.

Without going into too much detail, which would
hinder rather than help our present inquiry, it will
be valuable to show what this conviction about God
means as basic principle to live by. Without desiring
to be dogmatic we are able to assume that there is a
body of opinion sufficiently "accepted for substance
of doctrine" which is the inevitable result of the life
with God as Jesus knew it. There are some things
we know.

We know that this life, over and in which the
God and Father of our Lord and Master, Jesus the

Christ, is existent, is, in intent and possibility, a universe, not a chaos. You can find many who will disagree, but these do not belong in the Christian Church.

We know that truth is one, not many. Therefore we are not afraid to face any fact. Wherever an old concept has been proven false, we should rejoice as a scientist does, not weep the way the priest of tradition does, for we know that in the discovery of error we are that much nearer to the truth.

We know that love is a unifying force and hate a chaotic one. Since we know that, we must not pretend that we can reach the goal of a universe by using the weapons of its denier.

We know that this mysterious entity known as man is a personality of incalculable worth and unbelievable spiritual capacity. We marvel at the tensile strength of his matured and tempered spirit. Oh, yes, it snaps at times, either because man loses faith and hope in the purposed goal or because he is afraid for himself. But Angela Morgan's thrilling verse, called "Faith," is a part of our knowledge:

> "Though a thousand times I feel the thrust
> Of faith betrayed, I still have faith in man,
> Believe him pure and good since time began—
> Thy child forever, though he may forget
> The perfect mould in which his soul was set."[1]

We know that there is no peace for them that believe in God until the world deserves to be called

[1] Used by permission of Dodd, Mead & Company, Inc.

"The Beloved Community," wherein, to use Isaiah's words, "no one shall hurt or destroy in all God's holy mountain: for the earth shall be full of the knowledge of the Lord as the waters cover the sea."

All these things show the nature—the kind and quality of thinking about life—which made Jesus say by lips and life alike, "This is My Father's world."

People said, "How do you *know* that?" They had heard too many pious people say that "God's in His heaven, all's right with the world," to allow the expression to be used with glibness.

If you do not know when you say, "This is my Father's world," that this world as it is is not right; if you do not mourn because business is good these days for armament makers; if you do not suffer in your heart when you see a black face on the street because you sense how every doorway through which that face passes may bring fresh insult; if the searing agony which is existence for so many does not scar your own heart with pain: then you have no right to say, "This is my Father's world."

But He knew these things. This, at least, we know about Him. He knew Scribes and Pharisees and women of the street; the lame, the halt, the blind; a rich young ruler, Nicodemus, Zacchæus; Joseph of Arimathea, Judas, and Jairus; his jealous disciples, lepers and thieves, and a demoniac among the tombs; Rome and its tyranny, men and their envy: He knew —and He said, "This is My Father's world."

Then they asked Him again, "*How* do You know?"

And He told them: "My reason tells Me." This

does not mean it is something that you can prove as I proved that my centipede in the biology class had fourteen legs on each side. When you try to work man out in relationship with God and his fellow-men, you are stuck for that kind of proof. Man, as seen through the mind of one who needs a laboratory proof to believe in man as a child of God, is only "a physico-chemical organism, animated by external stimuli. Like an iron filing on a magnetic plate, he groups himself, according to the waves of energy which make contact with him. He is blind force moving in a world without meaning to no end conceivable." That is my description of man which I found in a college theme written for a philosophy course. Characteristic as it is of sophomore days, it still is a reasonable view of man. It checks with what we see: This aimless, drifting world with its lack of any apparent sense; this world which periodically takes the best we have and throws them out as refuse on the world's junk pile; this timid, tearful chaos we call civilization. It is not unreasonable for a man to look on the world and judge it has no meaning or purpose in its nature.

Yet it was on the same plane of the reason that Jesus went beyond what all men can see, even as truly great scientists go beyond it. He did not know that God is, as a mathematician knows $2 \times 2 = 4$; but He did know it as a musician knows that same fact, that $2 \times 2 = 4$, because only thus could harmony be. He did not know it, as a logician might prove that love is the world's greatest single dynamic; but He did know, as a poet knows, this same truth about love which the philosopher has worked out in logic. The world does not make sense as a chaos. There is no reason in it that way.

My reason tells me that this is My Father's world, is the way that Jesus made the first answer. And because it is My Father's world it hurts Me so to see the lies and thefts and hates—"the horrid shapes and shrieks and sights unholy." This is My Father's world. There is the end of war in this—some day. No one shall starve for daily bread—some day. My reason tells Me, was His first answer.

They said to Him again, "*How* do You Know?"

And He told them: My feeling tells Me.

It *is* reasonable to believe in God, the Father. One does not explain all things yet, to say this; but to say it is not so leaves too many things unexplained. But reason is not His only field of knowledge. He starts in reason, and ends in feeling.

Life is right when, believing in this interpretation of life, we act that way. This is my Father's world! Is it strange, then, that men who feel that, know they cannot take in their hands the tools of war again; or that they will risk their institutions and their lives, let success go by, give up honors they might have had, for such an unprovable value as a tiny seed of hope planted again in the corroded soil of an oppressed man's mind, a hope which may not bear fruit while he who planted it lives this brief span of time?

Life is not right—it does not feel right; you cannot trust it—unless, against the jungle law, you set the faith that this is my Father's world.

The idea of the Beloved Community is not dynamic knowledge unless behind it all and in it all God is a being at least as personal as ourselves. Not just a vague, impersonal spirit of truth and beauty and goodness; but God, the Father, witnessed to in this world by us, His sons and daughters.

Such a God is more than the all-powerful God of carefully planned theologies. He is greater than all-powerful because He dares to be less than all-powerful. He dares to give up His inflexible allness that man may have His chance to become like God. God could have made, as a man makes a watch, a world which goes on in unchangeable perfectness, adding myriads upon myriads of years to an existence without flaw, ticking on like a perfect machine, world without end. But the God and Father of Jesus the Christ is bigger than that. He made man a living creature. He flung the stuff of nature out into the world and set in the center of the universe an idea, unafraid that man, free to reject it, would not ultimately choose to be worthy to be called His Son. Man is no puppet on a string moved by the hidden fingers of God, no dummy in the lap of a ventriloquist God who asks the questions and gives the answers. God the Father, found at last as the dynamic knowledge of the sons of men!

To take your stand on this belief is no dead dogma. There is no statement more ridiculous than the one which says, "It makes no difference what a man believes; it's life that counts." It *is* life that counts, but man does *not* live without his great convictions. He lives, at moments, beyond them, but it is *in* them that he eats his daily bread and *from* them that he makes his ventures of faith. It is *upon* them that he sets his lever to move the world.

This sense of an unshakable foundation is essential to a truly effective life. It gives what we can well call "Defensible Frontiers."

This is a queer metaphor for a pacifist, taken as it is out of military strategy. But Jesus said one day in a parable, misunderstood as much if not more than any other, that the children of this earth are often wiser in their generation than the children of light. If the militarists, who are quite frankly the children of this earth, have discovered a truth about the nature of life, we should be glad to learn by their wisdom.

Empire builders have always known a truth about empires. It was Lord Curzon who stated the principle when he said that no empire could endure which did not have "defensible frontiers."

The phrase is obviously true. We must make it vivid. I find myself, when I hear those words, standing once more in the great Fort Vaux on Verdun's hills looking out of that narrow observation slit toward the German lines. There in the mud of the shell-chewed hillside I could see the flags which marked the place where that German fell who came nearest to the fort on the whole segment of that front. It was a waved line. As the waves of the ocean beat against a headland, so the German shock troops pounded that

citadel. They never submerged it. Up, up, they came
—receded; built on preceding waves the way an ocean
does until one wave ran far up on the shore—receded.
Up—up—up again—and left their futile high-water
mark lined in red upon the mud of those fields.

The storm ended and the fort still stood. As long
as any men were left to stand there, even as Horatius
on the bridge across the Tiber or as Leonidas at
Thermopylæ, it could not be taken.

This is a question the Christian needs to learn. There
are theoretical absolutes, of course. It is not always
easy to be sure what they are. But there are certain
practical absolutes, as well. Times and places where
a man says with Luther, "Here stand I, God help
me, Amen."

To have knowledge that nothing is able to separate you from certain ideas and attitudes: that neither
death nor life, nor angels nor principalities nor powers,
neither things present nor to come, neither height
nor depth, nothing can drag you below a standard
you have set. . . . To know that apparently for all
time certain temptations are safely held in their ex-
cluded place by the tensile strength of one's own
spirit. . . . This is one of the great joys of life. To
be not afraid when temptation recurs, knowing that
you have a life too full to allow it to enter, is to have,
in the empire of the spirit, defensible frontiers.

It is the empty life—the life filled with an unsure
hope—that has room for the seven devils to come in.
The Christian life must be rooted and grounded in
great convictions: not ideas wistfully used as possi-

bilities but convictions which have become an indivisible part of one's nature. We must know that in which we believe. It is important to be sure about that.

The life of power begins, then, in that feeling for ultimate truth which the life with God brings. Let's not forget, so that when it happens we may remember we were told about it, that the life with God is not necessarily comfortable. The peace of God is not a complacency.

When people find that out they react vigorously. There is almost a sense of being taken in, with some people, as if they had been tricked into buying something on false pretenses. That is a marvellous exit line of Susan in Rachel Crothers's play, "Susan and God." The shallow faddist takes up God on a "now everything will be lovely, all is sweetness and light" basis, but she finds that even on *that* level of concern God is not lightly to be taken. "Oh, I wish I'd never heard of God," she says with a touch of exasperated and slightly bitter bewilderment. And Jeremiah on the plane of a deeply concerned soul catches the same strain of an almost frightened sense of the inevitable God in his cry, "Then said I, I will not make mention of Him, nor speak any more in His name. But His word was in mine heart as a burning fire shut up in my bones, and I could not stay."

The life with God sweeps a man off his feet. You cannot tell where it will take you. Those who have known God have been "stoned and sawn asunder and tempted and slain with the sword." They have been in prison; and at stakes; and on a cross have cried aloud, "My God, My God, why?"

One of the things most difficult to stand when one enters into life with God is the queer feeling of lost control. Paul felt that about Christ. "It is not I that live but Christ who liveth in me." He cried, "It is a fearful thing to fall into the hands of the living God." He began many of his letters with the words: "For this cause, I, the prisoner of Christ."

No, life with God is not easy.

> "And I will give to thee man's work,
> So fitted to thy growth
> That in God's Kingdom building
> Thou shalt use thy largest powers.
> But this will cost thee both thyself
> And things which dear to thee
> Thou'lt lose."

The record of man in his contact with God does not vary in this fact.

Peter asserts the fact and makes the transition to the positive in his words to those in power who promised him freedom and safety if he would stop talking. And he answers: "Whether it be right in the sight of God to hearken unto you more than unto God you must judge for yourselves. We cannot but speak the things we have seen and heard." The life with God sets a man in the stream of life and he must run the rapids to the end.

But in Peter's assertion the positive side of the

experience of life with God is seen. When you recognize that life with God will not be comfortable—and I have never known a man who seemed God-filled who had an easy life—when you accept the obligation of sonship so that you know that you must be about the business of God, then into life comes power.

There is no need to argue that fact. This we know. Men who are in the grip of a Something they call God are at least not weaklings. They may not always be right, and they may not always be intelligent, but they do have power.

Knowing this fact—that the life with God adds power to this business of living—it is well for us to ask ourselves here on further question about Him. How does one keep that sense of Presence? I suggest three words:

First by *Withdrawal:* obviously this would mean what Jesus often did, going to the mountains, to the wilderness, to quiet places—to trusted and friendly groups. There in the apartness from the world one can feel what the poet said, "The world which time and sense have known, falls off and leaves us God alone." This is valuable and often essential. We get wearied by the pressures of the world and renew our strength in retreat from it.

But my concern is more with the how of finding God in the crowd. Jesus' withdrawal was so often without stopping in the work. He found God in the midst of the multitude. Remember the testimony of one who said:

"There is a viewless, cloistered room,
    As high as heaven and as fair as day,
Where, though my feet may join the throng,
    My soul can enter in and pray.

One hearkening even cannot know
    When I have crossed that threshold o'er,
For He alone who hears my prayer
    Has heard the shutting of the door."

To keep God's Presence we must find the cloistered
room. As many of you know, who have read my
book on prayer, *The Commonplace Prodigal*, my
chapel is the subway. Protected by its noise I am more
silent there than at any time in the day. By the curious
paradox of a crowd, the greater the number of people
the more alone you are. You must find ways to be
alone with the sense of Presence if you are to have
a life with God.

In that withdrawal comes the second action—*Expulsion*. This does not mean emptiness of life. It means
a *thrust*. Something pours in which will not mix with
what is there. Do you know *that* about God: That
you cannot have Him and keep many things you
might like? This was what worried the man in Francis
Thompson's "The Hound of Heaven,"

"I fled Him, down the nights and down the days;
    I fled Him down the arches of the years; . . .
(For, though I knew His love who followed,
        Yet was I sore adread
Lest, having Him, I must have naught beside)."

Let's not fool ourselves about this fact. Here is the

meaning of that expression of the Church, the *deadly* sins. There are certain things which shut us off from God. They are *not interruptions in the way*, not a slowing down of the time of arrival as a flat tire may interrupt a journey. Such things delay but do not prevent our reaching the end of our journey.

But some acts and attitudes become a determining catastrophe: a bridge down, a flood in the way, a mountain range through which there is no pass. Jesus did not say it is the impure in body who fail to see God. He was concerned about lives which had in the creative portion of their existence the iniquity which blots God out even as a red-hot iron plunged in the eyeball takes away the sight forever. We miss God because we think we can have Him and ———. It is that following list of things, irreconcilable with God, which makes us miss the power of life with God.

There can be no question that Jesus lived and taught this fact as a Source of His own Power: He that loveth father and mother *more*—who is concerned about institutions *more* ("In three days I could rebuild the temple")—"Let the dead bury their dead," "Sell all thou hast," "Seek ye first the Kingdom of God."

To be reconciled with God there must be the expulsion of things irreconcilable with Him. In that place of withdrawal we can know, if we have desire enough, that the things which keep us from the life with God can, by the expulsive power of our affection for God, be thrust from our lives. Part of the impotence of the Church comes in the fact that there is so little expulsive power in it.

The final word I hesitate to use, but know no simpler one. It comes out of the simple sciences we learned even in grade school: the phenomenon of *Osmosis*—or more accurately, the principle of osmotic pressure. It is the action of one substance mixing with another—permeating it, joining absolutely with it. And as the two touch, even though other membranes interfere, there is a pressure, seemingly against the law of gravity, lifting the substance, which by its nature left alone would not rise at all, until it is of the same measure as the substance with which it joins.

And Jesus, who began with the feeling, "I must be about My Father's business," ends with the knowledge, "I and My Father are one." There is a life with God which gave Him, which gives us, power. Men have found it so in all ages. We are going to need, in these days ahead, men and women who very quietly and surely know that power of life with God. The calmness in the soul, which is the gift of God to His own, is the power we shall need to help save the world.

CHAPTER SEVEN

The Inescapable Idea

*I*T IS fun to play with religion. You may know from your own experience how pleasant it is to be associated with a successful church and to feel from time to time the thrill of religion's ecstasies. But seeing what it can do to a man if religion becomes a serious business you had better be warned: do not let it get you. You can escape, on the one hand, by criticizing it, which releases you from a feeling of obligation; or better than that, you can erect the convenient barriers of plausible limitations against the obvious responsibilities which come from the Christian revelation of God.

There is an experience of a half dozen years back which remains in my mind as a vivid illustration of the way man plays at religion. I was seated by the lakeside on a porch, shaded with slat screens against the sun, doing some writing. Pad and pencil were in hand so that I was able to take down, word for word, as it was spoken, this soliloquy. Down the path to the dock came a little boy—perhaps seven years he had lived on this earth. He walked with that important air children have when they are playing at being their elders. He was "going fishing," as he had seen

71

his father go. He had no bait, but the rod and line were there and he could go through the motions. He threw the line in and caught a fish at once.

He pulled it out and said in a bewildered tone, "Oh, I caught one."

Hopefully he shook the line. The fish flopped but stayed on.

He held the line still, looking at it. The fish flopped again. Shaking the line impatiently, the little boy whispered hoarsely, "Get off! Get off, I say." The fish just flopped his tail.

After a moment the little boy put the fish back in the water again. The fish swam around pulling at the line. This time, a little more loudly, the little boy cried, "You get off there." But nothing happened.

Pulling it out on to the dock again, he kicked at the flopping fish. Still nothing happened.

"What'll I do?" He was now close to tears. He had hold of something too big for his experience.

Finally the fish flopped off. "There," said the boy as he kicked at the fish, sending it back into the water. He drew himself up with a long shuddering sigh of relief.

After a moment, he said, with a note of great satisfaction, "I catch 'em fast, I do."

He put the line in the water again. A fish darted over to investigate. Hastily the little boy pulled in the line, rolled it up, and stuck it over his shoulder. As he started up the path I heard him say, "I guess I won't fish any more today."

Be careful where you fish. There are habits of

thought, of action and inaction, by which we can play at religion without feeling its power. But you should be warned—it is a dangerous fever for a man to catch and one must be on guard with the plausible ideas of man's limitations if he would immunize his life against catching the real thing. The writer of Hebrews told us: it is a fearful thing to fall into the hands of the living God.

Men who have known God have never made final terms with the world on a basis of the world's interpretation of man. There has been always in a vital Christianity a sense of crisis. Never has a virile Christianity considered itself at one with the world in which it was. Always the true Christian has walked the ways of man with the consciousness that because he knew God—or was known of God—was in a certain sense haunted by God—he never could be quite the same as other men. This is not an easy idea to see and man spends a good deal of his time in contact with religion trying, consciously or unconsciously, to escape from it.

To realize that you are expected to be different from other men is too difficult a knowledge to be contained within the limits of duty. There has to come into any idea, if it is to be truly creative, a feeling. As James Stephens, the Irish essayist and poet, says in his *Etched in Moonlight*, "An idea may enter the mind and be alive; but it has no energy unless it sinks deeper than the mind into the imagination where abides the true energy of all thinking creatures."

It is the previous illustration of William Wilberforce which accents that truth. Privileged and comfortable as he was—doing good works at his convenience—he knew the facts and figures of the conditions of slaves in the British Empire. He could, however, file that knowledge away in the card catalogue of his information without letting it disturb his actions. "I knew," he said, "but was not haunted by conditions." It was only when he became haunted by the inescapable idea that God could not be reconciled with such a fact as slavery, that the unresting and unweariable urge drove him, without concern for his own failing health, to do the twenty-year-long job of eliminating slavery from the British Empire.

To do the will of God we must be held not by a command but by a concern. We obey God not because He says we must and we fear Him, but because we care for His way. Our minds flash back for a moment through our experiences of triumph and defeat as we think about this haunting presence, touching men's minds with the blinding glory of the idea of the perfect.

Not conceivably can God be satisfied with this world. Whether you think of the religious view of life in a purely individualistic sense, or in a purely social sense, or have made the essential osmosis of a personal and social gospel, no idea of God is adequate which thinks of Him as content. See the world even reflected in the mirror of God's face; or, if you can, get behind the eyes of God and look upon life. Can you think of a mind reconciled to you as an individual or this world as a community?

Before man—twisting and trying to escape—that inescapable idea moves. No man is quite happy until he faces the obligation of knowing God. It is no easy choice. Remember how Father Maple puts it in *Moby Dick*, as he preaches to the sailors out of the experience of Jonah: "O Shipmates," he cried, "if we obey God we must oftentimes disobey ourselves, and it is this disobeying of ourselves wherein the hardness of obeying God consists."

Now with all this as background for our thought, let us picture more closely this inescapable idea in the heart of man.

We are thinking now about the life of people to whom God is not simple. We do not forget the people who have apparently never known a doubt. We could not if we would, because inevitably when this idea of the haunting God is mentioned, directly or indirectly you can sense the bewilderment of those who seem always to have been sure of God.

There is a gentleness about some of these certain ones. They feel a sense of surprise not troubled by any understanding of how real your agony is when you cannot accept God without question.

Others, harder in their faith, show an arrogance, resentful and sometimes cruel. Your questionings, while not shaking their accepted belief, do make them aware of an alien world touched by a kind of insanity and explained by them as due to some wickedness there must be in you. Of such were the friends of Job and the masters of the Inquisition.

There are both of such among us—the gentle and

the arrogant—who have never known a doubt; and it will be difficult for them to understand why we are thinking about escapes from the inescapable God because they have long since stabilized life around moderate virtues.

For most of us, however, there is enough of the Hound of Heaven idea in our thought of God so that a responsive chord is struck in our lives of feeling and our lives of experience by the desire to escape; and yet we are caught by the strange sense of the Inescapable Idea which has haunted the life of man on the earth.

"It is a fearful thing to fall into the hands of the living God." One has a feeling that he must not let go of his own ways because if the Will of God ever becomes a real vision for him, he never can get back control of his life. Life is far easier without God.

There is a verse in the Psalms which expresses this idea. It is quite frankly a truth revealed by a shade of misunderstanding in translation and only the King James version has the text with this meaning. It is, therefore, as a truth which the psalmist hardly intended but which is nevertheless true, that I use this verse, "I remembered God and was troubled."

When the Inescapable Idea takes hold—when you find yourself unreconciled to your highest attainment because it is not enough to present before the holiness of God—when the unresting, unweariable passion of Christ's spirit revealing the mind of God gives you no peace in progress but only in perfection—you see then the reason why men try to escape. Faced with any worthy idea of God, men's minds are troubled. That idea will not let them rest.

An illuminating conversation between Charles and Barbara in John Galsworthy's *Worshipful Society* accents the agony of having to believe in God in such a world.

Barbara says carelessly, "Oh, Life is short."

She means thereby that we live a few years on this distracted globe and die by accident or design. When that incident or accident called death is over for you, that is all. You are then through. No feeling, no knowledge, no memory, no hurt or haunted sense of being. "Life is short."

And Charles replies: "Persuade me that it is, Babs, and I'll bless you. If we are pettily creeping on, furthering nothing, if there is no purpose in our lives, persuade me of it, for God's sake; for I'm haunted by the conviction that life has a meaning and that I must go on until I find it."

Do not let people persuade you too easily—as they will glibly try to—that belief in God is a wish fulfillment. I have sat too long listening to the heartaches of men and women to believe that. God is the Inescapable Idea. There are many pushed to the wall, who believe in God against their will and against their wish.

It is enough for now if you feel in your minds any of that trembling sense of possible discovery which a real idea of God gives. Some people, for example, who come up the steps into the Broadway Tabernacle, are conscious that above the door is a frieze of

Christ holding out His hands to the multitudes; and there comes into the mind that awed and trembling sense which is the beginning of true worship. A man feels a hesitation because he hears a still small voice saying: Perhaps today you will see God. You may feel Him as once you did—and have since forgotten all but that memory of Presence. You may see Him, perhaps, as you never have seen Him before—an immediacy—the urgency of the perfect.

It is this direct sense of relationship which is so powerful but which is so disturbing to many people. They are disturbed, some of them, intellectually because they cannot conceive that the power behind the universe could have any concern about the minutiæ of this world of humanity. But far more disturbing than this sincere bewilderment about how one can believe intellectually, is the awful sense that if one ever does let go, he could never again gain control over his own life. He wishes then he did not know the inescapable idea of God.

But there is no "power to become" unless, in the world we know, we feel this tug on our daily living. A world with God is not easy. It is an abandonment of yourself to a mighty current beyond your control when you launch your life on the stream of God's truth. But having once been touched by the Inescapable Idea, the world without God is cold and dead and empty. Men try to follow goodness but find when the sun goes down that they lose their passion for perfection. The breath of life is gone from the body of the world when ethics is man's highest guide and God is not his goad. Then, because he will not face Him, or when he forgets and fails to find Him, there comes the Dark Night of the Soul. Troubled though man is when he remembers God, it is far more terrible to find life without dynamic because he has feared to let the idea take him to whatever end it will.

Augustine said it centuries ago. "He hath made us for Himself and our hearts are restless until they rest in Him."

God is more than all-powerful. He dared to make life a matter of man's freedom to choose, rather than to make man a machine which either does God's planned will or breaks. But in that free world in which God placed man, He also set the Inescapable Idea of Himself. No man's life can avoid, sometime or other, facing that fact.

The daily life is far easier if we can forget or fail to feel. But I crave for you that troubled sense which life with God gives. Life reaches its real joys only when we have faced the ways used in trying to escape from Him, and when we give ourselves without reserve to our hopes and thrust after the perfection He makes us care about.

CHAPTER EIGHT

God's Finger on the Scales

THERE is probably no question harder to answer satisfactorily than this. What does God do in this world? The last chapter may have given you the idea that God is taking care of everything and all you have to do is to give yourself over to Him in some absolute but after all indefinite way. To try to answer the question, "What does God do in this world?" may save us from a very common but dangerous error in thinking.

Does He care about the world—does He care about me? If He does, why doesn't He do something about me and the mess I'm in—about the world and its despair?

Does He interfere in events—affecting results by getting into the situation and changing things? Well, if He doesn't, what good is He? And if He does, why doesn't He do it now? This is a good chance for Him to change things.

What are we trying to do in prayer? God is—whatever else He is—fundamentally honest. Are we asking Him to be dishonest in putting His finger on the scales?

If that seems like a lot to try to answer in one chapter, at least it will give you some idea of what a man who says he believes in God is up against these days. They are tense, highly emotional, and very insistent questions which people are always asking and which fall under this beginning and ending question, "What does God do in this world?"

The first thing we say is very positive. Yes, God cares! About the world? Yes, there can be no ultimate doubt of that. About you—me? We hesitate a bit more this time. We are not able to prove this. Sometimes it seems that He does not. We ask, how can He? And yet if He does not care about you and me, how do we explain reasonably the life we live?

We do not say God cares without our being conscious of the immensity of the world we live in. I quote from a letter a college girl sent me, expressing vividly her inability to believe that this world, in which she believes God is purposive intelligence, can be bothered about her. "Honestly," she writes, "can you sit down and think of the space that 100,000 light years means and then say 'There is a spirit who has a little place reserved for me'? I just want to beat my hands out against the sky and say, 'No, no, there is no such thing,' and yet—" and then she drew a long dash and gave it up for the moment, quoting a poem of John Hall Wheelock, "Loneliness without End."

"Between the immensities of heaven and ocean
    My spirit's thought makes forward falteringly.

. . . .

In the vast reaches of His meditation—
The sorrowful distances—her stricken wings
Flag, failing her. My heart's imagination
Faints, in the lonely endlessness of things."[1]

This is a reasonable mood. If you did not have it,
now and then, we could almost question your intelligence. But purely on the plane of man's finiteness we
look at a man who cares and one who does not care
about what goes on around him in the world.

Here is a man in a world where he feels, he knows
not why, a responsibility for others. The world feels
right when an individual lives on the belief that man
has fulfilled his highest possibilities when he is willing
so to live that he will give up his life for his friend.
The world seems out of joint, somehow, when people
starve or freeze or have no chance to develop as other
men with work and play and family and friends.
There is dynamic in that belief: A man has to do
something about the world.

Then the voice of doubt comes in. Nobody cares
what you do. It makes no difference anyway.

Is war upon the face of the earth? It is as inevitable
as flies buzzing about a bit of carrion in the summer
heat. Does race run riot on the streets, does a grim
mob gloat over a black man's sizzling flesh? They are
black ants and white contending over their hills of
dust. Do classes engage in industrial conflicts? Just
spiders and bugs struggling in cobwebs in the corners
of tumbledown buildings.

[1]From *Poems*, 1911–1936.

This doubt produces a man who begins to think it does not matter and who ceases to care. What happens? We see men acting on the belief that God does not care; that man is on the earth "to get his"; that life is a struggle for self-existence on the plane of an educated animal. Much is to be said for this rationally. But life has lost a feeling of being right when this doubt about the nature of God's world shrouds him.

Then we see a man—maybe the same man with faith regained—acting on the belief that God does care; that what a man gets in things or so-called success in this world or any other world is not important; that life seems right and true when a man gives up his life for his friend. Something in the cadence of the universe responds to that sort of living. Terror departs. He walks the earth with lighter step and higher head. We conclude that there is something true, something in tune with the universe in the life which results when man lives in the confidence that Jesus' revelation of God is valid.

This happens to a man who cares about the world: There is a sense of meaning and purpose to life, and power is evident in him.

This is no proof that God cares. I am simply asking you to consider the known difference in values in a man who cares and one who does not. Then look at the fact, which scarcely any of us doubts, of the unknown, but surely to us infinite, power of any God who could be purposive intelligence behind this universe. God may care differently about this world from what we do. It is quite probable that He does.

But He does not indifferently watch the world. This is our basic belief. God cares.

Well, if He does, why doesn't He do something about me—about the world? That question sends us into the second major issue. Does God interfere with events? My positive answer would be, that if you mean interfere in the way most people pray about it —no. You may remember that old song about the huntsman chased by a bear who climbed a tree only to discover that the bear climbed better than he. Out on the end of a limb with no place to go he prays: "O Lord, if you can't help me, for goodness' sake don't help that bear."

In that tragi-comic incident we can vision what we do to God in expecting that He was waiting and watching for the time when the danger point would come, and just before the bear bit the man He interposed His protecting hand. Meantime, of course, do we say He is watching a surgeon's fingers in a New York hospital because a man has prayed, "Save me from death," and is guiding an unemployed man's feet to a certain door where he can get a job?

We do not believe this with our highest moral sensibilities. It is only in our facing a desire for favor that we hope God will change the facts for us. The world is an insanity with a God who could, and some-times does, change things because He's asked, but otherwise leaves us hanging on a string. Remember Mio's bitter words in Maxwell Anderson's *Winterset*, when some one says something about the concern of God for those in trouble. "So Jesus cares for his sheep, does He? Well, I've seen some lambs that Jesus missed."

It is a terrible dilemma you force us into if you say God does interfere in events. If He does sometimes, why doesn't He now? Is not the world frightened enough of the mess it's made? Are there not enough children crying in the night; enough sinners who weep the bitter tears of remorse; enough sorrow for those "loved long since and lost awhile," for Him to act? What holds back His hand from a hundred changes we could set down which would make a better world? If He could change things but does not because nobody asked Him, or not enough people asked Him hard enough, He is not as moral as the least of us. There must be some other rule than mere caprice which makes God withhold His hand.

If God is responsible for patching up this world, we would not blame James Thomson for writing:

"Not for all Thy power—furled or unfurled,
  For all Thy temples to Thy glory built
  Would I assume the ignominious guilt
  Of having made such men in such a world."[2]

But the process of bringing this world to the fullness of the idea that was in the Mind of God is not a tinkering. I once believed—I hope I never do again—that God interferes capriciously with the world He has made. I learned in the trenches the meaning of the expression, God causes His rain to fall upon the just and upon the unjust and the sun to rise on the evil and the

[2]From "The City of Dreadful Night."

good. Thank God we live in a world of law and not a world of caprice. How can I answer a mother mourning for her child or a black boy unjustly shut up in a jail, if God can and does change the world for another and does not for them? Quite apart from making Him petty, it makes Him immoral to make this an untrustworthy world. God keeps His finger off the scales.

This brings us to our final and topic point: God's fundamental and unshakable honesty.

This point around which our thought centers is a vital one for us all. God chose to make man free—a moral being with responsibility for his acts. He could have made it otherwise—this world of ours. Sometimes it seems as if He had—that it was all somehow in His hands and we were puppets on the string, having no will of our own. One of my favorite quatrains is from the Negro poet who said:

> "Sometimes it seems as though some puppet player
>   A clenched claw cupping a craggy chin
>   Sits just beyond the border of our seeing
>   Twitching the strings with slow sardonic grin."[3]

But in my sane moments I know that Browning told the truth of this mystery when he said:

> "God who . . . brought
>   Man into being, stands away
>   As it were, a handbreadth off, to give
>   Room for the newly-made to live,

[3]Angelina Grimké, "The Puppet Player," in *Opportunity: A Journal of Negro Life.*

And look at him from a place apart,
And use his gifts of brain and heart,
Given, indeed, but to keep forever."[4]

Popes may claim that God has spoken through them as Moses claimed that God's finger wrote the words on the stone he broke, and which in another sense man has broken ever since. Lesser men may claim that the will of God is discoverable with a pencil and a blank piece of paper and an equally blank mind. If that is the way God works, He dictates some strangely contradictory commands.

How different the world becomes if you do not use God as a Great Switchboard Operator. Tell me! we plead. The Spirit of the Eternal answers: There is the book of life. Read it. Here is the Christ, the incarnation of the Word. He knows our temptations, this Christ, but He exhausted the possibilities of sin without even having to go through it. Here also is a prodigal, wasting the substance of life in riotous living. And God's finger did not turn him back. There is no morality in this world unless man chooses, on his own, without interference. There is the book of life. Christ, and the prodigal and the elder brother. Nicodemus and Caiaphas. The whole of it is open for you to read and for you to understand. God has power to tip the scales—to destroy the balance of a trustworthy world. But He won't. He is bigger than a dictator giving orders. He is big enough to control Himself—to have power and not to use it. To use it would be to deny man's freedom. Morality is to have

[4]Robert Browning, "Christmas Eve."

power to destroy yourself and to choose not to. And God, who made a world where man is this being of moral responsibility, does not weigh His own finger on the scales of judgment or of decision, for that would be to deny the fundamental honesty of that world His hands have made.

What, then, does God do? people ask again at this point. "You have taken away all the things I've been praying about." I am so sorry for a person when that is said, because it reveals how little has been experienced of this God who touches life with daring and calmness, with peace and with power.

God has laid His hand upon you. Not His finger on the scales but His hand upon you. "You are Mine," the Spirit of the Eternal says to a beaten, twisted, wasted life—"You are Mine."

"Thou shalt not be afraid," He says to one walking in peril of the night and of the day: Pestilence—shell splinters—temptations of the body or spirit—doubts of the mind. "All that is real; but My hand is on you. Thou shalt not be afraid. There is no place so high, no hell of despair so low—no loneliness so far, where I am not," says the Spirit of the Loving Father. "I have laid My hand upon you."

This is a constant. No special guidance—no interference with the right to choose—nor with the necessity of reaping what you sow.

Some people think God does not do very much if He does not do what they ask. Is it nothing that a father loves his child; is it nothing that a friend stands by a friend; is it nothing that His hand holds the stars in their courses, and sets beauty in the heart of man, and gave you the chance to become, and honors you and respects you by not interfering with your choice? Do you want in addition that He shall keep you from going too far sometimes and protecting you from having to go to crosses? Christ prayed in the Garden, "Let this cup pass from Me." He cried upon the cross, "Why, Why?" But He had chosen to face life as He did. And God honored His choice. He kept His finger off the scales.

We sometimes say that the pharisees killed Jesus. They did not. His passion for perfection killed Him. His concern for the world killed Him. He could have knuckled under. Stronger men than He had done so before and will again. But Jesus felt the hand of God upon Him and He marked indelibly across the mind of the world the truth about God. God does not interfere with the world He has made. He keeps His finger off the scales. And He does it because He has done something far greater than to use His power for our purposes. He made man in His own image— a being free to reject the world or to choose life. There is meaning to the words of the hymn we sing: "Be still, my soul—the Lord is on thy side." He has laid His hand upon you.

CHAPTER NINE

Glory of the Lighted Mind

WE ARE, at this point, in the place of greatest danger for religion. It has been right to begin the question of the sources of power by the thought of the life with God, the Inescapable Idea. This world is too big for us unless we go back to an adequate concept of the power behind the universe. We are too weak ourselves, our visions are too narrow, our sense of futility too inevitable unless we believe in the greater-than-ourselves. Until we feel the Something There, we do not find in ourselves the power to contain the world. The world gets you down when the Knowledge of God is absent.

With that knowledge, you can look upon the world without dismay. "I see what you see," said little Studdert-Kennedy in one of his poems and went on to list "the lies and thefts and hates" which turn the mind of man sick with futility. To see God does not shut out, it rather reveals even more clearly the world, its sickness and its sorrows, its suffering and its sin. *Because* one has seen God, he can no longer stand the world that is. And one makes no final compromise with the world that is, because of the confidence in the world to be.

All this one can find in God, but not by some inevitable "process." It should be obvious to any one
who has seen much of the Church world, that knowing God, as men do sometimes know Him, is not
enough. That can be a very pleasant and comfortable
matter—a Holy of Holies, a peace-in-the-sanctuary
experience. It is the kind of experience which is to be
deplored since it makes of religion an opiate rather
than a dynamic.

The life with God can be then a false and futile
thing unless to some extent you have seen the world
—felt the agony and the need of the world—tasted
the sour reality of it—heard its groans which could not
be uttered—smelt the sewer gas of its woeful waste—
lain crushed and helpless under the weight of its
inertia. And it is often that a man does not really
know these things until he sees them in some moment
when he no longer believes in God.

There are times when, quite apart from God, and
I mean literally that: being without God—you must
see the world if you are to find the life of power.

Sometimes that experience comes outside your control as when some great tragedy overwhelms you or
some unexpected doubt takes away your faith. Sometimes it is an act of intelligence whereby with a disciplined imagination you face the meaning of the real
world of time and the times. But until you do manage
to see the world in its hell of despair, in its sewer of
degradation, in its treadmill of futility, in its prison-
house of fear, you are inadequate to serve it well.

It was Victor Hugo, in *Les Misérables*, who stated

the principle when he said: "We may feel a certain amount of indifference to the death penalty. We may refrain from expressing an opinion; from saying Yes or No, so long as we have never seen a *guillotine* with our own eyes. But when we have come across one in action, we must decide either for or against."

King Lear illustrates it further, as he felt none of the tragedy of the poor until he was in the storm himself, and then his prayer pours forth:

> "Poor naked wretches, wheresoe'er you are,
> That bide the pelting of this pitiless storm,
> How shall your houseless heads and unfed sides,
> Your loop'd and window'd raggedness, defend
>   you
> From seasons such as these? O, I have ta'en
> Too little care of this! Take physic, pomp;
> Expose thyself to feel what wretches feel,
> That thou mayst shake the superflux to them,
> And show the heavens more just."

"It is seeing it yourself that makes the difference," said one of the men who had caused the death of Joan of Arc when the clergyman asks him, "Were not the sufferings of our Lord Christ enough for you?"

The sufferings of Christ had become for him—or rather had never been anything else for him than—a phrase in the sanctuary to which at an appointed moment he had murmured a response. It was seeing a girl actually burned to death which released a hidden dynamic in him. And it is seeing the world that makes the difference between knowing something with your intelligence and understanding it with your feelings as well.

Seeing the world means then that we must realize its tragic contrasts—realize and be unreconciled to them.

Our realization begins in recognizing the fact that this is a segregated world. Cruelly, tragically, but unquestionably it is so. This is a segregated world. We do need to hold constantly before our unwilling consciousness this truth even though it is an unpleasant and terrible fact.

Without desiring to be unpleasant about it, but knowing that the only chance for a cure begins in an honest realization of the facts, we must think about areas of experience in which segregation is a commonplace.

We become so familiar with our own lines of cleavage that we are as if blind. The culture that was Greece thought as little about the slaves which made possible her comfortable philosophies as do we remain conscious, except by effort of imagination, of those who make our stage of civilization possible.

There is a poem called "My Lady of Leisure" which, after recording with stunning detail the fingers and faces making possible my Lady's leisure, ends with the line: "Which build her inconceivable and fragile shell."

It takes something a little removed to make a principle stand out. We see the appalling uselessness of my Lady's life. We may have missed a relatively vast and insensitive unconcern in our own acceptance of the worlds men live in. Our only hope is that seeing the mote in her eye we may be able to guess that we have a beam in our own.

Let us see if we do see, by wandering through some old French Quarter as any tourist might. It is interestingly historical—curiously different from the world one knows. Suddenly one finds oneself in the Red Light district as any tourist might. I would to God you could have felt with me the spiritual agony of that storm of realization.

One day I walked along a road on the Verdun front from Haudainville to Belrupt when a sudden bombardment sprang up. There was no shelter. Beside me a building rose in the air and came down in ruins. Like the flick of an angry driver as his whip took pieces from the hide of his beasts, the hissing, snapping "éclat" clutched at me. With a terrible tightening of my whole being, I walked along. How long would it last? To stop was fatal. Just behind my step, a piece of shell bit into the ground. To hurry was useless. Just before my step, another piece of steel came down. I simply walked along. Then as suddenly as it came, the bombardment was over.

Like that one walks through several blocks of a Red Light district and then the voices are no more, no shuttered door peeks open. It is a respectable street again.

No more? Yes, one. Almost as a symbol, there comes a haunting echo. A shutter opens and one looks back surprised that a voice should speak again, and sees a slight little girl, a figure clothed all in white, ghostlike in the darkened street. Out from the edge of the segregated into the area of the respectable, meaning to be attractive, there is this pitiful, pathetic, symbolic daughter of our Father's world.

I am against a segregated district to isolate the age-old problem of prostitution, as I am opposed to segregation of races to allow a white civilization to pretend that this is our Father's world. But this is not a treatise about the perversion of the potential beauty of "male and female created He them." This is but another illustration of a segregated world.

Let no expediency of "it-is-better-for-my-class" blind us to the dishonesty of complacent segregation in a world which prays "Our Father." The nationalistic trends in government, the growing tension of lives in the class struggle are but further evidences we need not do more than mention of a practical denial of a positively expressed faith.

Let's not be soft in our thinking about these facts. To say as some men do, "if only men would love, these things would not be," is sentimentalism. Life is not so simple that we can love it into a certain success in any given measure of time. There is a bit of verse, whose lines I cannot recall in full, which tells of some bold bad man who drew a circle and shut you and me out of his world. The poem finishes "but love and I had the wit to win. We drew a circle and shut him in." It is too glib. There was shut into that circle a foreign body. Love, when it includes hate, feels often like having a cinder in the eye—a cinder which cannot be ignored.

This means that there must be in our perception and presentation of the truth of Christianity an exactness of understanding and a sharpness of action that cut. It is important not to forget that the Christian life needs a cutting edge, as Jesus told us clearly in that statement, already mentioned, "I came not to send peace, but a sword." Read in its context it is evident that Jesus was talking about the divisive character of the truth. I came to divide you from father and mother, from son and daughter, from all your loyalties and responsibilities, if need be. This is the supreme loyalty to let the knife edge of truth fall where it should, cost what it may. Let us take one manifestation of this truth.

Religion is of no dynamic value in the world unless it makes its adherents aware that there is an inevitable segregation in life no matter what we do. It may not be—certainly we would say it is not—an ultimate part of the practical nature of the universe. But it is an inevitable part of that practical nature now, and unless we realize that fact we are conventionally moral people without being truly religious. Religion must do more than make us act conscientiously. It must, as Professor Oman says, "seek an ever more penetrating consciousness."

Any life, therefore, which has in it a redeeming quality—redeeming of itself and redemptive for society—must have in it "a program of discontent." (The phrase is Whitehead's.) This is essential to any sane strategy of Christian living in such a world.

Now discontent, like satire, is a dangerous instrument. In blundering or unskilled hands it can destroy rather than cure a sick world. But with that necessary caution about its possible destructive effect, the statement still stands.

It sounds queer: the hope of salvation for the world lies in a program of discontent. Yet this is the only possible attitude for a religion of perfection. This, strange as it sounds, is the reaction of the optimist.

They are the pessimists, not believing in any deep foundational sense in themselves, or man, or the world, or the God whose holiness they profess, who stabilize life at arbitrary values. Cheerfully content are these, satisfied—in such a world as this—to give one tenth of their income, to go to church twice a week, and to keep within the laws. This is no world in which a decent man has a right to rest content. The contented man is fundamentally a pessimist.

It is the optimist, believing fundamentally, positively, hopefully, in beauty and truth and the perfect life, who remains forever discontent with this life we know until the Kingdom comes.

Do you remember the first time you realized that men, women, and little children were caught in the relentless grinding of a machinelike industrial system which had power enough to take from the backs of struggling humanity much of the burden of poverty? Yet they were held there not because it was necessary in nature, but because some were afraid of losing their privileges, and, in their unwillingness to use their power, created an artificial scarcity in the midst of plenty to sustain, or to attempt to recover, a false prosperity. Have you become so used to it that you say, "Oh, well, that's the way of the world," or are you still searching with a hurting sense of your own sin to discover the processes by which our power may become the door of opportunity to the abundant life for every one?

The tragedy of the commonplace religious life is that it becomes reconciled to a temporary inevitability. One of the long-time absentee members of the church asked one day to be dropped from the rolls because he said that we had made him see that he was not a Christian.

"The ideal of the Christian religion will not work now," he said. "Maybe thousands of years from now it will; but my children will not see it, nor will their children, and that's as far as I am interested. Life is always going to be a fight, and selfishness and Christianity do not reconcile. I can see no hope of the church changing this condition within the lifetimes in which I am interested and I am, therefore, asking to be considered no longer a member."

Far better than a soft and sickly sentimentalism, his attitude makes a line of cleavage clear. The tragedy is that the ideal he admits is true, if the world ever is to have sense, is abandoned as a practical part of his life because he sees clearly the inevitable segregations of the present. His discontent with what is was swallowed up in his discouragement. To be unreconciled to the imperfect destroyed his peace and he preferred to withdraw into his own computable world.

Jesus told us what to do about our world. It is seg-

regated. He did not deny it. You must be in this world
only you cannot possibly be of it, was the constant
emphasis of His lips and life.

If, then, we are to see the world we must keep ourselves close to human need. "Live close to human
need!" This does not mean only the sordid. It is true
that the ache of the world's sorrow and suffering, its
sordidness and its sin, makes for strenuous living.
When things begin to speak to you so that you see
blood on the coal you shovel into your furnace to
keep you warm, and tear stains on the shirts you wear
to keep you clean, or on the dresses which make you
pretty, then life loses a certain simple and placid joy.
But in that loss of bliss which comes from ignorance
we find a power we fail to see when all is comfortable
for us.

When people begin to represent to you not only
themselves but their problems, when buttons and price
tags become alive with meaning, recall how Jesus
clothed simple things of life with symbolism. If you
do not remember, read again in the New Testament
about what He did to coins, and sheep, and children;
to roads, and journeys, and pieces of broken bread.
When sounds become sermons (do you suppose Nicodemus ever listened to the wind again without thinking of an evening conversation with Jesus?); when
two sparrows chasing a crow or a mother partridge
in the woods pose the problems of the nations—all
this and more too make vivid what a terrible thing
it is to have an imagination. You are never able to
be unaware of the interrelated world.

Do you realize further how much harder it is to live close to those needs that are high? This is the reason why the suffering servant of Isaiah was so difficult; why the cross is such an agony. We but touch the outskirts of His ways. The power of the cross comes in later, but for this moment we recall that the poet told us how:

"All through life I saw a cross,
Where sons of men yield up their breath.
There is no gain—except by loss,
There is no life—except by death,
There is no glory—but by bearing shame,
There is no justice—but by taking blame."

It is here, I believe, that we discover the strange exceeding power of religion. Seeing the world, which all who have eyes they are willing to use can see, puts into the life of any sensitive soul a horror. And out of horror comes determination and out of that follows power. The mass of life takes on motion and, you remember the formula of physics, $M \times A = F$, Mass times Acceleration equals Force, so your sight produces action.

But the friction of the world defeats the power which comes from horror alone. Here is where you must see not only the world that is but see clearly the world which is to be.

You can become accustomed to horror. But you can never be reconciled to ugliness of spirit, to lowness of life. It is they who have seen beauty who are forever haunted. Thornton Wilder in a book you should reread—*The Bridge of San Luis Rey*—explains why the artist is never satisfied. The actress and her friend and coach, old Uncle Pio, are not content with her position as "the best." And the writer with his poet's mind interprets: "Whom were these two trying to please? Not the audiences of Lima. They had long since been satisfied. But we come from a world where we have known incredible standards of excellence, and we dimly remember glories we have not seized again. And we go back to that world."

The man who sees the world and fights it out of horror is satisfied when he sees progress, but he who sees the world and fights it out of the consciousness of potential beauty is not satisfied short of perfection. This is what some people missed seeing in Sean O'Casey's *Within the Gates*. They saw a prostitute —while O'Casey was trying to make us see a child of God.

This too is what statistically minded people miss in what we hate in war. A letter came to my desk one day asking why I was so concerned about the waste of war since more people are killed by automobiles each year than we of America lost in the World War. But it is not numbers of lives which are killed that count. It is not death we fear. It is the waste of life we care about.

Be clear in your minds about the words waste of life. My concern here is not with loss of bodies which can be numbered: so many units dead of which war caused X lives lost; Automobiles $X + Y$; Cancer $X + Y + Z$. It is the dead still walking the earth

who are war's tragic waste. They no longer believe
in anything. Without faith or hope or love, they pass
through *the days of our years*, the living ghosts of
men whose lives, in the full meaning of life, were
taken captive by the one who sat on the red horse
of the Apocalypse. These dead see the world which
is and find nothing for which they believe it is
worth while to live. They no longer see the world
which is to be. They have lost the hunger for perfection.

It is a terrifying power, this instinct toward perfection. Some day it may tear you apart as Jesus was
broken upon the cross. Seeing the world which is
is bad enough, but believing in the world that might
be is life's greatest agony. Yet there is no power like
it. It gave Jesus the strength to see it through to
the end.

It begins in the Life with God. That opens one's
eyes to see the world. Walter Rauschenbusch, in his
spiritual confession which he called "The Gate to
God," ends with the thought:

> "Is it strange, then, that I love God?
> And when I come back through the gate,
> Do you wonder that I carry memories with me,
> That my eyes are hot with unshed tears
>   (*for what I see*)
> That I feel like a stranger and a homeless man
> Where the poor are wasted for gain,
> Where rivers run red (*with the blood of young
>   men*)
> And where God's sunlight is darkened by lies?"

That takes away the placid peace of men and will make you forever restless on this earth. But it gives you power, as you see it, to set yourself indomitably against the world for Christ's sake.

"But when He saw the multitudes, He was moved with compassion on them, because they fainted, and were scattered abroad, as sheep having no shepherd. Then saith He unto His disciples, The harvest truly is plenteous, but the labourers are few: Pray ye therefore the Lord of the harvest, that He will send forth labourers into his harvest."

CHAPTER TEN

Let's Be Realistic

EOPLE are always saying, Christianity must work. And of course it must. Unless it is workable, unless it is a practical and reasonable matter which some day will be, we *are* just kidding ourselves. Religion becomes a pathetic thing—a solemn little song and dance which means nothing unless it *can* and *does* work. To have a world of lies and thefts and hates; to live on in fear and unsatisfied hunger, and never to have it anything else is just too silly for words. If the book of Revelation is only a pretty dream in which there comes the vision of the Holy City where nothing shall enter in which defileth or causeth an abomination or maketh a lie; if Isaiah's majestic tones are merely an orator's rotundities as he cries, "They shall not hurt nor destroy in all God's holy mountain, for the earth shall be full of the knowledge of the Lord as the waters cover the sea"; if right is ever to be on the scaffold, wrong always on the throne; if gangsters are to get away with murder, be it on the civic or the international scale; if there are always to be wars and rumors of wars, riots of race and class; if the poor are always to be with us world without end—then indeed Chris-

tianity is a denial of truth. Christianity must work
—and it can work now.

But when people go on to say that it must necessarily in this moment of time, in this particular situation, and for me, work now, we set up at once in
protest the clear witness of Christ's life and teaching.
No! There is no obligation upon Christianity to produce in the distorted interrelationships of men a mi-
raculous new world in the twinkling of an eye.

Maybe God *could* do it. It is not a very practical
matter, but if you think it important, let's say at once
that He could. But He doesn't. He won't. And He
can't unless He gives up the idea that man, in this
flesh of ours, has in himself the possibilities of the
divine; that you as a man have it and could completely
choose to do the will of God now; that you have
what it takes to pay the cost. There lies the crucial
point. Has man the power to choose God? Is he able
to consecrate himself and make the painful journey
back from the far country of individual and corporate
sin?

When people say, "Christianity must work and
work now and if it does not work now I'm through
with it," they are not understanding what Christianity means. We have a glaring example of this in those
who claim that Christian pacifism has failed. They
say, "Look at Italy and Ethiopia, China and Japan,
Hitler and—" to mention any specific country dates
the illustration, so pick your own. "Unless pacifism
works now to stop Italy, Japan, Hitler; and to bring
about an immediate peace, it has failed."

I wish emotionally that this were true. It makes life so much simpler than it is. We all like to have life simple and it would be so much easier if the critics of pacifism were only right in their simple alternatives: "Does it do the job now? That's all you need to ask. Then O.K. I'm for it. If it does not do the job now then it is no good and I'm through."

If there is an obligation for Christianity to work now to stop Japan (to pick one continuing situation) and it does not—as it is not—then you and I, you see, are released by this false simplicity from an obligation on our own part to be Christian. Christianity has not worked and so we are now free to do what does work. Let's get mad at Japan, let's just erase all the places where it said Germany in our speeches and sermons during the last war and write in Japan: beast, gangster, mad dog, barbarian. It will help us to forget when we boycott Japanese goods that, natural and even necessary as it may be to fulfill by some definite action our individual sense of decency, we are, nevertheless, starving little Japanese babies by our act.

This does not refer to embargoes on instruments of war. But starving out a population is a different matter. No, no, protest the crusaders for the Holy War: It is the Japanese militarists who are doing that.

I know and we are helpless to prevent it. But if you do cut off their food because you feel it is a military necessity, do not forget that we are thereby a party to the sins of the war lords. Whatever else you think, do not be so sentimental that you fail to see that acts of boycott which result in the starvation of populations are at least no Holy Crusade. If they are done at all, it must be in the clear consciousness that because we have all of us sinned, we have come to this moment of time. It is our failure that Christianity, which must work—might now be working, if we had believed in it when we should—will not work in this moment of time. Remember also that it will not work in the *now* of some tomorrow unless we, believing in it, do not lose it in ourselves today.

Christ never told people that succeeding now was the test of the gospel. He did make clear to them that the way set before them often led in an exactly opposite direction from man's experience and instinct. "Love your enemies." "Do good to them that despitefully use you." No wonder Paul called it, "to them that perish foolishness; but unto us whom He saves it is the power of God."

The tragedy of time and of our times is that churchmen forget what they are. They speak as if they were statesmen having on their shoulders the responsibility of military victory. Whatever else it does, the gospel of Christ never has made that demand.

Recall how Jesus sent His followers out to convert the world. He made it clear to them that it was a gospel of perfection. How perfect it was is shown by the startling demands it made. You think you are righteous because you have not killed. I say unto you, he that hateth his brother is a murderer. You think you are pure because you have not committed adultery. I say to you, how have you looked upon women? And with that demand that His way could be and should be lived by men, He said, "I send you out as a lamb among wolves." Later he said, the time will even come when they that put you out of the Church will think they are doing God a service, and I tell you what I see so that if and when persecution comes because of the gospel, you may remember I warned you that it would happen. Your job is to live out the word. Talk to people about peace—this peace which comes from God's way. If they receive you—well, but if they do not—"let your peace return to you."

This is the place where so many of us fail. Christianity, you see, has two beginnings or angles of approach. It begins in an idea: a principle, a goal, an accomplished perfection, an act of faith that there is

> "God, *Who* ever lives and loves
> One God, one law, one element
> And one far-off divine event,
> To which the whole creation moves."[1]

This mood we often hold in spite of contrary evidence. In that mood we feel the—

> ". . . unhurrying chase,
> And unperturbèd pace,
> Deliberate speed, majestic instancy,"[2]

of the God in Christ.

There is a limitation in this because, so long as one individual stands outside the love of God—in that much the truth is denied. There is no more tragic nor realistic picture in the Bible of the reason why

[1]Alfred Tennyson, "In Memoriam."
[2]Francis Thompson, "The Hound of Heaven."

the Kingdom of God has not come than is that unwilling, unseeing figure of the elder son who had
never gone away to waste his substance in riotous
living in some far country of obvious denial of the
good, but who stayed outside the knowledge of his
father's love in all the time we see which the story
covered. Christianity which must work and can work
is always short of the fact so long as one person is
outside the truth.

This, however, is a situation not difficult to face.
Placidly we may say with the poet:

> "Yet I doubt not thro' the ages one increasing
>   purpose runs,
>   And the thoughts of men are widen'd with the
>   process of the suns."[3]

Or one says in undiminished confidence with Jesus,
"You will not do it now (follow Him) but you will
afterwards." Here a man can walk with calmness.

It is in the other beginning where the pinch comes:
if they receive not your witness, let your peace return unto you again. Here is the obligation of the
Christian to believe in and live out a Christianity
which does not work—now.

We catch the beginning of this essential mood in
Ecclesiastes when that so-called gloomy preacher says
to a cynical world, in which he himself sees no signs
of progress: live good anyway! That which you feel
in your heart is true. It does not make provable sense
but it is true nevertheless. God made everything beau-

[3]Alfred Tennyson, "Locksley Hall."

tiful in His time and set that world in our hearts and
there is nothing for us to do but to do good with our
lives. Give a portion to seven, the holy number, and
also to eight, for one cannot tell whether this or that
will prosper or whether both may come alike—good.

Wells says the same idea in a more specific situation
in "The Tale of the Comet," where he pictures the
armies in the world when the comet passes by. As the
soldiers are facing the renewal of the conflict, one of
them looks up at the stars. "If only we could build
something in this world," he says, "to fit that." Paraphrase that idea: here is this stuff of existence, tremendous in its possibilities. If only we could fling out
against that background something worthy of it—
something that would not clash with it as these war-
ring worlds do. Then the tail of the comet passes
over them and men fall into momentary unconscious-
ness. Some of them are not affected long. Some come
back to consciousness more slowly than others. But
each man, as he comes back, has a chance to think.

It is probable, says the observer, that if they all had
come back to consciousness at the same time and
found themselves dug into opposite trenches with
guns in their hands, they would have begun to fire at
each other from sheer inertia. Sometimes things go on,
you see, not because men are mean or desire evil but
because of lazy minds—the utter inertia of spirit. They
just have not really thought what they did.

They thought, if they thought at all, that it was
something they had to do. But in this brief sleep of
the comet's tail, they wake up slowly and each man

had a moment to think. And each man knew in that moment that *he* could not shoot. The gun in his hands seemed silly. It had no place in sound sense. It was an absurdity in any decent thought. Nothing could justify its use. To take that piece of organized power and let it smash in the face of a fellow human being, just could not make sense. With a loathing sense of horror, the soldier dropped his gun. Whatever any one else did to him or to any one made no difference. Suddenly he knew that he could not shoot.

You see it was not a question of whether it worked. It was a question of whether it made sense—of whether it was right—of whether it was a part of truth.

That old best seller of A. S. M. Hutchinson's, *If Winter Comes,* has been in my mind these days as I have seen from several angles the mystery of the victory of the spirit in the lives of individuals. You know this business of the Church would be impossible to stand in its slowness if we did not see from time to time the evidence of the truth we stand for actually ruling the life of some individual. Dorothy Canfield makes the remark that the thing which embitters life is the sense that unrighteousness is triumphant. Well, it does seem so. And you would quit unless you sense, now and then, the assurance of the ultimate failure of unrighteousness by watching the hold that love can take on this weak and wobbly piece of flesh man seems to be.

There, in Hutchinson's story, is Mark Sabre, clerk in a publishing house, who has been so terribly

wronged by Twyning, one of his superiors. Twyning
—so well named—with his petty officiousness has made
Sabre's life unpleasant enough for years. Now by his
whispers and his insinuations, his nods and shrugs, he
turns the villagers' minds against Sabre, who has had
concern for poor Effie and her fatherless child. Sabre
takes her into his own home when the father turns
her into the street and no one will take her in.

There is nothing else to do, is the way he feels. His
wife leaves home but still Sabre cannot turn Effie
out. One cannot just turn an outcast girl into the
street because it will avoid trouble.

Then Effie commits suicide in trying to eliminate
Sabre's problem, only to have him accused of influ-
encing her to take her own life.

Tried and grudgingly acquitted of technical blame,
Sabre goes home from that horrible scene in the court
with no one left to believe him decent. He discovers,
when he winds the clock, the letter from Effie which
names Harold Twyning, son of Sabre's detractor, as
the father of her child. Harold Twyning had marched
off with the village regiment and was now at the
front. The story is all there in the letter.

It is a very natural reaction Sabre. has. He grabs
a cab and starts for his enemy's office: I'll show him.
I'll cram this proof down his throat. I'll bash him in
the face with it.

He rushes into the office of his enemy. He holds
out the letter of proof. He is about to speak; and he
sees that Twyning's shoulders are bowed over a tele-
gram. It is from the War Office. Harold Twyning

has been killed at the front. Sabre hears Twyning's voice: "Oh, my son—my only boy—my Harold."

Sabre's hand drops. He goes over to the fireplace and tries to think: but it's my life in this accusing world against the good name of this boy, and he's dead and the son of my enemy.

Sabre turns and starts to speak. Suddenly in his mind there come the words, "He that dwelleth in love dwelleth in God and God in him, for God is love." Slowly his hand crumbles the letter. Quietly he holds it over the fire and lets it go. Gently he pats the shoulder of his helpless enemy and goes out to face the world in which his Christianity has not worked for him. But His peace returned nevertheless to his spirit.

This does not prove anything in any law court of the land. It is not enough for the bar of public opinion to have faith in the way of Christ when, in a world which is the result of an accumulation of evil choices, war breaks out. But it is enough for one who, facing the kind of world we have, has come to believe in the ultimate triumph of God's truth revealed in Christ. That person knows that Christianity, which must work in the end if it is the truth it claims to be, does not need to work now—and especially not for me, now.

This is not an easy idea to live. Nevertheless this message, which we claim is the good news which will save the world, will affect the world only if it makes us see this something which is different, something clearly divisive as far as the world's ordinary standards are concerned. Moreover, the idea must be evident in the way it makes those who profess it, and the world which makes contact with them, attractively different as personalities and as a community of people.

We must be very sure, therefore, that we are realistic in the application of our Christian thinking and the action of our Christian lives toward the world we live in.

At this point we are up against one of the world's most slippery words. People are always trying to settle an argument by saying, "Let's be realistic." It is one of the standard ways of making a black-white, I'm-right-you're-wrong world.

I do not mind the phrase so long as we really *are* realistic. But realism demands that we define our goals, make clear our sense of fundamentals, reveal first of all what we want. Then we can see whether we are being honest and intelligent in our ways of getting it.

Take, for example, the people who come to my church. What they are wanting, presumably, is to find out what it means to be a Christian and how to live Christlike lives. That being so, realism means: how do you take what you have and use it so that it accomplishes what you want to do?

The Church *then* must make them realize that unless they never give up an ideal they believe to be the truth, holding to it even though apparently they are failing in it, we and the world are lost. When we become deceived by the appearance of demonic possession of the world, and I do not deny that appearance, we must be realistic enough to face this fact: there is no victory in climbing up a stepladder when you are seeking the secret of how to fly above the clouds.

Let our minds play upon that idea for a moment.

Let's begin by denying what many people carelessly assume is the rule of the universe: that what happens is determined by what came before. Cause and effect it is called in physics and psychology.

This is an orderly world, men say. It has sense to it. It is not just blind chance. There is a purpose behind this universe. Such being the case, we build, they say, on what has been; effect follows cause; that which was done yesterday affects action today. That's the way life goes on. Be patient! We are making progress. Out of causal sequences will come at last the Kingdom of God.

We should challenge the carelessness of that assumption: that what happens is determined by what came before. We say instead: events are determined by what is to come afterward. Naturally we would not maintain that this is true in all things. But it is true in the big things and it is true in the creatively determining things. The things which happen now happen as they do because of what is to happen afterward.

This has such a queer sound to it, almost as if we were calling black white, that we need a very concrete and obvious illustration lest we become confused. It comes in one of my most comforting experiences in trying to be very practical.

A man came to me who needed bread for himself

and his family. Obviously he needed not words about the abundant life, but a job. But I have no jobs for men's hands to do that they may get bread. I am one of these impractical men, you see, who deals with ideas and ideals which are nice-sounding but which do not solve practical problems—or at least so men tell me.

But this problem looked easy. One of the men of my church had just been appointed as construction superintendent to build the Sterling Library at Yale. I had been by that great hole in the ground which was all that was left of a whole city block of dwellings, stores, and college buildings which had stood there. There is the solution, I said to myself. A new project just starting requiring work by many hands for many months. I'll go to this man of practical affairs and he will solve this practical problem which is beyond my power as a man of ideals.

I stood beside this hard-headed building superintendent who had a ten-million-dollar project in stone in his charge. I knew men's hands must put these stones in place and so I told him confidently of my need.

"I'm sorry," he replied, "but we have no place for workers here."

"No place for workers on this big building project?" My astonishment was evident.

"No, not yet," he said. "The time for workers has not yet come. You see we have no plans yet by which we can build. All we have now is a picture."

"Do you mean to say," I said, "that you tore down

all those existing buildings and made this hole in the ground merely because you had seen a picture?"

"Of course," he said. "We have to get ready. When those who are working on the blueprints to make the picture possible are finished, then we can begin at once."

Is he crazy? Is he a menace to the stability of our world because he tears down what is and digs a deep and ugly hole in the ground on the promise of a picture? You can answer that question yourself. But the present point is that the event of destroying those existing buildings was caused by the building standing on that spot now, which came afterward and which was at that time only an idea—a picture drawn by a man who dreamed of what was to be before it was. I grant you that the idea came first, but it was an idea about a future event. What happened to those buildings was determined by what was to come afterward.

Do you see now why I say that there is no victory in climbing up a stepladder when you are seeking the secret of flying above the clouds? It is not realistic to be timid, cautious, "to keep your feet on the ground" when you are trying to prove you can fly. Ladders and wings are in different realms of ideas.

The concern of religion and life then is to ask the question, Whom do you serve? What do you want to accomplish? What is your object? Settle that. That determines what you do. Realism is being sure that what you do now will not leave you sitting on the top of a stepladder at the end of your endeavors, reaching out futile hands to the still distant stars.

My generation was told, "Fight this war to save democracy and end war." That was realism in 1917. Left sitting as we are on this precarious stepladder of the present world, we need to rethink the meaning of realism now.

Is not this then the supreme tragedy of man's sentimentality about religion, the final irony of life, that he exists so often by the very opposite to that which he has sworn is truth and as he does so he says, "After all, we must be realistic"? You and I must charge the world with the keenness of insight of a more valid realism.

I know no finer statement of that than Victor Hugo's comment in *Les Misérables:* "We so often deny," he said, "by our way of attaining the goal, the meaning of the goal. We strive for an ideal tomorrow by borrowing, as the process of attaining it, from the falsehoods of yesterday. We do not put our faith in the irresistible and incorruptible strength of our principles until after we have made ourselves secure on the world's past falsehoods."

This world is going crazy with fear. It is for us, who believe in God, who have confidence that truth cannot be defeated, who have not given up the nature of man to the pessimists, but who believe that He is capable of building at last on earth a community in which justice rules and no man fears his neighbor—it is for us to be realistic enough to use now this religion we have professed, and use it more than ever in these times when everything else is going down before that realism of expediency.

You may not believe in God. You may not believe that Christ's Way is the ultimate way of the world. But if you say you do, be realistic enough to know that when you have the least apparent chance to win, you must the more calmly give witness to the words you have with your lips professed, because that is the only way the skeptical world will ever believe that religion has power to affect the life of the world.

CHAPTER ELEVEN

Practical Christianity

$\mathcal{T}$HIS is a plea for a practical Christianity. It will not be what some of you might think, because, far from advising that we go slowly, being sure that we can carry the slowest along with us before we move, it is a plea for the very opposite.

There are many people in the Christian Church who do not really believe in the Christian gospel, and the attitude has so often been, among so-called wise heads, that we must wait for those to believe before we can go forward. The Bible strongly says the opposite: "What if some did not believe? Shall their unbelief make the faith of God without effect?"

One of the places where the world is astray at the moment is in talking of "practical" as if it were a noun —a word describing an object which is what it is, meaning the same to everybody. "This is *wood*," we say as we touch a table. "This is *cloth*," we say as we touch our garments. "This is *practical*," we say as we touch upon some idea. We are almost unconscious of our shift in the use of words. A great deal of our mental confusion—political, economic, social—comes from the fact that we use an adjective as if it were a noun.

We are thinking of Christianity, and the particular kind of Christianity is a practical one. There are other kinds. What we want to know is, what, from the Christian point of view, is the practical way to live; what are the practical things to do?

You and I have no right to continue using our time, energy, resources, in this venture of the Church unless from its standpoint we can make an effective influence upon the world. But what is practical Christianity will be obviously impractical from other points of view. For the Christian, if he is a practical Christian, not just a sentimental one, must do some things which would seem mad to those not Christian.

Obviously, a Christian is not practical from the standpoint of a pagan. I use that term in the sense of the detached, the fundamentally disinterested person, who does not care what happens, so long as it does not happen to him. Ibsen's Peer Gynt was a pagan. He says it this way: "Know ye what it is to live?—It is to be wafted down the stream of time, wholly, solely for oneself." Modern nationalists are pagans. Hitler is quite right from his standpoint in persecuting the Church, because the Christian Church has in it the seed of victory over his nationalistic philosophy. As did Nero, so must he, from his own practical standpoint, subdue the Church, if he can. He should, however, read the history of the results of the Neronian and other persecutions if, even from the point of view of being practical, he faces realities.

But your pagan—whether professedly a Christian, as some of them are, or whether he is a more honest, or at least keen-minded, pagan, and knows himself not to be a Christian—uses practical in a different way from that in which we are using it here.

Obviously, a Christian is not practical from a politician's standpoint. The man who is a politician in whatever realm he operates is a half-a-loaf-better-than-none man, the man who has his eyes on the expedient, the immediately possible.

This man bargains with life for the best he can get. A thorough Christian is just stupid to him. When Gandhi in India started his non-violent non-cooperation movement, he had told his followers that they must not in thought, word, or deed, be violent toward their opponents. This proved too great a strain upon the flesh of those who were not thoroughly indoctrinated with the ideas of the movement. Even as many zealots followed Jesus for a while, so many who hated England followed Gandhi for a while. But when the police used clubs, even as Peter in the Garden snatched a sword and started to defend Jesus, so the non-violent non-cooperation adherents became violent, stick-using, window-smashing, head-breaking combatants. Twice the order went out to begin the campaign of non-violent non-cooperation. Twice violence became prevalent among Gandhi followers. At once he called off the strike against England.

"That is political suicide," men who knew the workings of the mob mind said. "Once he can do it, but not twice. He had victory in his hands. He might have brought England to his demands. But because he was squeamish about the methods, he lost his chance."

That which is the only practical thing for Gandhi to do, if he remains true to his beliefs, seems to the politician stupidity.

Obviously, a Christian is not practical from the standpoint of a man who believes we should preserve existing institutions at all costs.

In Walpole's *The Inquisitor,* which finishes the Polchester novels, the life of Ronder, the ambitious church politician, comes to an end.

Ronder is now an uninspired mechanic for church machinery, oiling the wheels of the Cathedral as he coasts fumbling and ineffectual through the middle years. Having power, he does not know what to do with it. His passion burned out in getting power, which he has no passion to use.

As he nears the end of his life he realizes that he has missed life's meaning somehow, and he talks with a young curate named Gaselee, in words which remind you of Wolsey, "Had I but served my God with half the zeal I served my king." Ronder tells the young clergyman that away back in the beginning he took a wrong turn.

"I've lost something I might have had that a real churchman has," he said.

"They have something we haven't got. They have intensity. They may be wrong, but they *believe* they are right and fight and sweat and pray for what they do believe. Don't you see? Either this whole thing, the spiritual life, is nonsense or it's real. It must be one or the other. If it's nonsense, what rot this all is and has been for centuries! But if it's real, what are we doing about it? Have you attended an ordinary church lately? What do you find, nine times out of ten? A droning mechanical service without thought or meaning. An unreal sermon with a lot of dead symbolic phrases taken for granted. A mumbled repetition with a lazy choir and a scrap of a congregation. *If* it's real, don't you suppose that some one is angry somewhere?"

"I feel myself to be held in the hands of the Great Inquisitor. Looking me over He says, 'No life here. Nothing worth preserving.' And He tosses me away, and it is too late to do anything about it."[1]

It is not too late. Certainly it is not too late for us. We are not too old, too set in our ways, too bound in timid traditions, or fears for self. We care enough about Christianity to want it to win. Maybe we are not yet willing to lose ourselves that it may win, but we want it to win. If we did not want it to win, to make a plea for a practical Christianity would be senseless.

But—it is wise to be sure that we see what we mean when we make a plea for a practical Christianity. We are trying to see clearly that to seek first the Kingdom of God makes some definite and practical demands upon a Church and upon people bearing the name of Christ.

[1]Hugh Walpole, *The Inquisitor*, pp. 212–13. Doubleday, Doran and Company.

For a practical Christianity means, as it always has meant but particularly now must mean, such supremacy of loyalty to its cause that nothing else is even arguable.

Two areas in which that loyalty makes its demands I shall now suggest. Emotionally, I take the harder first, though actually, when the testing time comes, the order is likely to be climactically harder as we go on.

A practical Christianity will not preserve the nation if we do it at the expense of Christian principles. In this first area of abstract principles we find the basis of the early Christian persecutions. The simple early gospel was clear on this point: that the Christian was first a citizen of a universal Kingdom.

This may seem treasonable to the nationalistic patriot, it may seem visionary to the hard-headed business man, it may seem stupid to the politician, and quixotic to the pagan, but it is practical Christianity.

Over on the Western Front one day, months late, I received my Christmas mail. In it was a letter from my church, urging me to remember my home and womenfolk and to be a good soldier of my country —and of Jesus Christ, the last almost an afterthought. Enclosed was a little printed card containing the poem by Howard Arnold Walter called "I Would Be True." My eyes ran down the familiar lines,

> "I would be true, for there are those who trust me;
> I would be pure, for there are those who care;
> I would be strong, for there is much to suffer;
> I would be brave, for there is much to dare."

There is strength, power, the sense of the inevitable cross in it.

"I would be friend to all the poor and friendless," came the words of the next line. I stopped aghast.

"Why?" one might ask, "are you not willing to be friends with the poor?" Oh, yes. But you see Howard Arnold Walter had written the line, "I would be friend to all the foe—the friendless." We were at war, you see, and it is treason to love the foe in time of war; and so my church, urging me to be true to the Christ whom I had professed, created an armistice on the gospel of love and substituted the poor, who are always with us.

The Church must never do that again. Whenever the world driven by fear or imprisoned in futility is so lacking in intelligence on the one hand and spiritual insight on the other, that it sends out its boys to stick bayonets through the soft bodies of other boys because their governments or their businessmen could not get along together, we must not let any false ideas about saving this institution of the Church for some far-off future service to humanity lead us for one moment to neglect those principles for which that institution was founded. And face this squarely: because I used war as an illustration, do not forget it is only the particular example of the whole range of human experience which confronts us today. It was Ibsen who once remarked, "The greatest enemies of the people are those who hold the safety of its institutions above the principles of those institutions."

A practical Christianity will not preserve the

Church unless, in it and by means of it, people see God. Fumbling and frustrate though we often seem, the Church is still blazing trails and building highways.

The Church is not a monument to God. It is a movement for God. Unless it does its job of showing people a way to live, and helps, by changes in the organization of society and in the attitudes of individuals, to make that way possible to walk, it will have saved its institution at the cost of its life.

A practical Christianity therefore is sorry, but not worried, when its institutions are endangered by its principles.

A practical Christianity seeks first not the nation's safety, or its own security, but the Kingdom of God.

The other area in which a practical Christianity has its demands today is in the personal realm. Has the world ever called you mad? It is God's madmen who have saved the world. Can you imagine Abraham's friends when he announced what he planned to do in leaving all to obey God? "Seventy-five years of age, and starting out all over again to give substance to an age-old hope! Why, he's crazy!"

Or Moses. Jethro probably said, "Moses, don't be a fool. You are my successor in the best sheep business in the county. Forget the slum-dwellers of Egypt, those brickmakers of Pharoah!" But Moses had heard the voice of God in the cries of men.

There was a carpenter in Nazareth. His father was dead and trade was good. To make true houses, and smooth ox-bows, and neat coffins, and to live in the respect of his fellows: this He might have done. But steadfastly He walked the way that led Him to that ghastly failure in time—the Cross.

Now let us be careful lest we give an impression He would not have wanted. There are those who imply, and these very illustrations could support the idea, that to serve God is to go some place other than where you are, and to do something else than that which you are now doing; to wander in sheepskins and goatskins, being destitute, afflicted and tormented, having no place to lay one's head.

This seems to me to be a superficial requirement for living as children of God. He did not ask this of Zacchæus, nor of Nicodemus. He told the man healed of a devil to go back to his own home and people and live out his new life where he was. No Christianity is practical which does not redeem the whole world.

If by chance you are persecuted for your faith; thrown out of your job for your convictions; or ostracized for your opinions, you must be careful lest you "rejoice and are exceeding glad" over that which may be only a martyrdom of escape. We do not prove the truth of Christ by creating opposition but by winning acceptance. We must be sure that we make the "dens and caves" of lost causes but tabernacles in the wilderness set up for the moment as we keep our eyes fixed on the City of God which is to be.

We do not, however, redeem the whole world by waiting until all the world is ready to go forward.

It is impractical Christianity to seek for the power of this world.

With full reverence, my mind moved in imagination the other day to the meeting of Jesus with God after the crucifixion. "He ascended into Heaven," so the creed puts it. He was face to face with God. And God said,

"So You failed to make men see My way."

And Jesus answered, "Nay, Father, they saw so well that they crucified Me."

"But You failed to make them want what they saw."

"Nay, Father, they could not contain their wanting it, and, lest it destroy them, they crucified Me."

"But You failed to make them know they could contain it, failed to make them know themselves to be My children."

"Yes, Father, in that moment when they crucified Me, I did fail, but in that failure I shall forever haunt them 'til they come unto Thee."

Then said God, "My Son, return unto the world I gave Thee. And do not return until they come, reconciled unto Me."

And Jesus returned unto the world.

If, then, we are to be practical Christians it means that we must not wait for the world. The Church is suffering today from the fallacy that progress is made by waiting for the slowest to move. The Christian moves with the Christ. Where He stood, you must stand, alone, if need be. It will take you into ridiculous places, link you with queer companions, cause you suffering at times, and you will lose much dear to you. But Jesus knew that the only practical way to follow the guidance of God's spirit was to follow it. And you and I will not do His cause a service if we forget that it is only when we hew to the line and let the chips fall where they may that we are being practical from the Christian standpoint.

CHAPTER TWELVE

How Can You Tell If You Are a Christian?

Y FIRST ANSWER to the question set before us will sound a trifle strange coming from one who is concerned, as I am, with Christian social action. Rightly we emphasize the truth in Christ by asking what a man does: "By your fruits ye shall know—" "By this shall all men know that ye are My disciples if ye show love to one another—" "If ye know these things happy are ye if ye do them." "Thou hast answered right: this do and thou shalt live." The texts are almost without end. It is action that is the test of a Christian.

Nevertheless my first answer to the question, "How can you tell if a person is a Christian?" comes in this: by what he says.

Action is by no means the only test of a Christian, because action can be as deceitful as words. Attitudes are more important in the eyes of God than acts. Guard yourself at this moment against thinking that it does not make any difference what you do just so long as your heart is right. Such a division of right and wrong is not possible. I am not justifying an unintelligent wrong act merely because the man meant well. What I have said is that the *why* is of as great importance as the *what* in considering whether a person is a Christian. And it is speech that tells, or tries to, about the why of action or inaction. A scene in Peter's life is stretched beyond its obvious meaning, to be sure, but can be taken as symbolic of this truth.

Peter was standing in the court of Pilate—silent. By no act was he showing himself to be a follower of Christ. The fact that he had followed to the court meant nothing. Lots of curious people had followed the excitement. It was when he spoke that a fact was revealed.

"Surely thou art one of his followers," the serving maid said. "Thy speech betrayeth thee."

Insist upon a literal and obvious meaning if you like. It was his accent. It was his dialect. As one might say, on meeting a stranger, "I'm glad to meet some one from Scotland," although no word about Scotland had been said, so you may say they knew Peter for a Nazarene.

But all inhabitants of Nazareth were not disciples of Christ—far from it. A prophet is without honor in his own country. This is just the carpenter's son, so many of them had said, as they did not hear Him. We might argue the point. But let's not. Have it the literal way if you like. It was just Peter's accent that made the maiden say, "Thy speech betrayeth thee." This is all that the account actually says.

For you and me, however, it has a symbolic meaning. If you want to know what a person is, let him talk. This does not mean take down his speech. This does not mean to hear him when he is careful. It means listen to him speak. Catch the spontaneous outpouring of his mind; his asides, his give and take reactions, his quick comments. Listen for example when one mentions a name.

Out of the many which stir men's hisses or handclaps in the newsreel houses, let's take one. You name him; the labor leader currently most hated in the clubman's world.

"Some one ought to shoot that man," was what the voice said. It was said loudly, openly in the lounge of a fashionable club.

"Yes, and I'd like to be the one to do it if I got the chance," was the response from one of the men in the group.

Now, of course, he wouldn't. He was still a small boy fighting pirates with a bravado which would not be challenged by any real pirate. But his speech betrayed nevertheless what he was. Jesus said, "It was said unto them of old time, thou shalt not kill; but I say unto you—" and then the principle of a man's attitudes was brought in. He that hates bitterly, unjustly, this one is a murderer though he never takes a life. He that looks with unclean eyes on a woman or a man is an adulterer, though no act is committed.

Do you see that the man is a murderer?

"Oh no, he's not," some people will at once react. "It's what men do that counts."

Let's be sure you mean that. And in being sure let's turn from murderous thoughts to words of promise extravagantly expressed.

"Though I die with Thee, yet will I not deny Thee." Was it what he said or what he did that revealed Peter?

Here is the principle pictured in the life of Jesus with His friends when He has told them that the testing time is coming, and realistically Jesus has faced the fact that He cannot win at that moment. Little children, He says to them, I'm going away—and whither I go ye cannot follow Me now. But you will some day. Meantime don't be afraid. Don't lose your nerve. Don't fail in your faith. Don't let your joy be taken from you. Peter said, "Lord, why cannot I follow Thee now? I will lay down my life for Thy sake." Jesus said, "Will you lay down your life?"

Interpret now, off the record but in the spirit of Jesus: Peter, dear friend, I believe you would lay down your life. You would die for Me. But that's not what I'm asking. Will you take up your life for My sake? Will you live for Me? Oh Peter, you don't realize how you are going to be tested. I'm not asking you to die gloriously for Me. I'm asking you to live unpretentiously for Me. Not their lashes but their laughter you must face. Peter, good friend, don't look so troubled. I see into your heart. The words you say, you will not do—now—but they betray you to Me.

Thou art a rock upon which I shall build My Church and the gates of hell shall not prevail against it.

Now which was right: the extravagant promise of what Peter said or the weak act of what he did in Pilate's court?

Here we can look on the record. Fortunately we have it. Remember later how Peter lived. See him standing amidst the sneers of men. Watch him as the mob menaces—as the men of power threaten him (the word "threaten" is in the record). "Whether it be right in the sight of God to hearken unto you rather than unto God," the quiet words come from Peter's inner life, "you must judge for yourselves. We cannot but speak the things that we have seen and heard." "And seeing the boldness of Peter and John they marvelled and they took knowledge of them that they had been with Jesus."

Who was right: Peter who wept because of his weakness and thought himself no good because of his acts? Or Jesus who saw in his speech what Peter really was and was justified later by the way Peter lived?

In that thrilling picture Browning paints of David's attempt to help Saul out of his mood of despair we find this truth I seek to have you know, clearly expressed. "Then the truth broke upon me," David cries and goes on to speak of his impotent yearning to help, of his desire which is beyond his power to make effective, of his conviction that somehow the universe is meant for perfection and that this idea of the perfect could somehow—if only he knew how—

"snatch Saul the mistake, Saul the failure, the ruin
he seems now—and bid him awake . . .

> "From the dream, the probation, the prelude, to
> find himself set
> Clear and safe in new light and new life,—a
> new harmony yet
> To be run, and continued, and ended—who
> knows?"

"I believe," he cries in ecstasy. "What stops my
despair? This. 'Tis not what man Does which exalts
him, but what man Would do." Then the poem ends:

> "And the stars of night beat with emotion, and
> tingled and shot
> Out in fire the strong pain of pent knowl-
> edge; . . .
> And the little brooks witnessing murmured,
> persistent and low,
> With their obstinate, all but hushed voices, 'E'en
> so, it is so.' "

That is valid. Over and over again we have seen
it. Man is not just what he has done in any moment
of time—that "still" which men sometimes take of
the moving picture of life. Man is what he cares about,
and thinks upon and loves. What a man is, therefore,
is betrayed by what he says. His speech reveals the
direction in which his life is moving.

If you don't see why that clubman was a murderer already in his heart, there is no use arguing
about it. You have to see a thing yourself, you know.
Annette, the French newspaperwoman, said in Ro-

main Rolland's *The Soul Enchanted*, during the war when the community ostracized her for being good to a German prisoner, "One does not argue with a stone wall." If, therefore, you do not really see how important the casual speeches of people are, then no argument can convince you.

Let's look, however, at another thought which may reveal the importance of this point. One of the arguments often made in "bull sessions" about religion and life is on whether you could really call anything a belief which did not control action. "How can one say he believes in anything which he will not or does not live?" is the way one objector stated it. "You either believe a thing or you don't. Why kid yourself into thinking you believe something when quite obviously you do not mean it?"

Now the trouble with that comment is that the objector was thinking only of the fruit and not at all of the seed. It sounds so logical but violates a feeling —denies something we do know.

There is scarcely a person who reads this who cannot discover some present conviction which has been a process of growth so gradual that it would be difficult to tell when the belief became dominant. Are there not, in your life's experience, uses you now make of energy and money which formerly were but casual interests of your convenience? Once you could take them or leave them alone. Now they are dominant concerns.

Have you failed to have the experience of realizing that there were some things you cannot do without violating the whole meaning of life for you? Yet you can look back, sometimes only a short period, to the time when the question would hardly have become an issue for you. Somewhere back in your experience, the details of which you have forgotten, is something which touched your mind, was examined by your reason, was spoken about casually, became a subject of thought, was an opinion you said but on which action was postponed, then a haunting idea, and suddenly you wondered why you had not always felt as you do now.

You can tell whether a person is a Christian by listening to what he says, by seeing where his accents fall, by the things he picks out to emphasize.

The famous story of the Gadarene swine is an example of this. Jesus went across the lake to a section of the country where He was not known. The first thing that happened was that a man, possessed of an idea which made his life an insanity, met Jesus, and Jesus healed him. It was one of those startling transformations of life Jesus was always doing. In the excitement of the crowd, some people said Jesus had sent the devils into the swine because a herd of pigs stampeded down the hill and were drowned. Whether there was any causal connection is not the point. These are the facts: a man was made whole; some pigs were dead.

When the people of the village came out to see what had happened they were told and they saw both facts: a saved man; some lost pigs.

It was what they picked on to talk about that is

disturbing. They talked about the dead pigs. It was not to be the last time that people would talk about dead pigs. That men, who had been driven to insanity by the life they lived, were now given a chance to live decent sane lives, was not what they remembered. "That's all well and good," they said, when the new life for a poor man was pointed out, "but how about our pigs?"

You can tell whether a person is a Christian by what he says. "Surely thou also art one of them; for thy speech betrayeth thee." You can tell about yourself by the words coming unbidden to your tongue, by the thoughts that spring irrepressibly to the surface of your mind.

There are some words from Jeremiah which make a proper ending to this section of our thought about the way of Christ.

If you have been touched at all by the passion of Christ's spirit there have been times when in such a world as this it seemed too much to bear, as "the word of the Lord" was too heavy for Jeremiah. Nobody cared. Why worry about it? Why not give up —struggle no longer against the lethargy of men's minds, the self-centeredness of their lives? Granted that men are basically good and that the universe is on the side of righteousness; nevertheless they do nothing and evil prevails in our time.

Then said Jeremiah, "I will not make mention of God nor speak any more in His name." What's the use? is the idea. We talk and talk and talk and nothing happens. We pray and pray and pray and this is what we have on earth. Then the prophet tells what happened to him. He tried to keep still. But "His word was in mine heart as a burning fire shut in my bones, and I was weary with forbearing, and I could not stay."

We need not be discouraged about this world. In the sadness of my generation's war experience, I remember how I searched for the way which will save the world. I heard some people who were at least saying what I believed must be: that God was the Father of us all and all men are brothers; that so long as any man was bound no man was free; as long as any suffered adversity we were one with his suffering. I saw what happened to ordinary men under the impact of the Word made flesh and dwelling among us. I said, I will go with them—the men and women who say these things. I can tell that they are Christian because of what they say. I shall see if together we can do what we say, that the Kingdom of God may come.

But there is a second answer to the question: how can you tell if a person is a Christian? Into it is poured all the desperate longing of prostrate souls—the hopes and fears and high desires of people without number who have felt the passion and the power of Christ's spirit. This on the one hand. On the other there is all the common sense of an outside and skeptical world. Both skeptic and enthusiast rightly answer: you can tell whether a person is a Christian by what he does.

This is not a reversal of the first answer: you can

tell a person is a Christian by what he says. We still say that life begins in those ideas which have the power to direct or cause such an action. Long before action comes you can tell what is in process of happening by the words a man uses. This is disturbing sometimes. I sit on lots of committees. Every once in a while my heart thumps with distress as I hear a man express an attitude about some matter of policy or make a comment on programs. Something has happened to him and I fear he is lost to the Kingdom. The vision is passing away and fading into the light of common day. Something has hurt his courage, or touched him with fear, planted in him the seed of doubt about whether Christianity works. Something has confined him to this world; made him think like men. He has become "in harmony with chaos."

On a certain board on which I sit there is a man of considerable influence and fine promise. The man who heads that board came to me in distress some two years ago and said, "I can't depend upon Blank any more—what's happened to him?" "I don't know," I answered, "but I knew it was going to happen. Over a year ago I chanced to be with him at an informal luncheon party of businessmen and from his casual comments on things going on in the trend of the common life, I knew he was lost to us."

By what a man says you can tell what the set of his life is, the direction in which he looks, and the place at which he will arrive if he moves at all. It cannot be emphasized too strongly; words are the seed in the soil of life. Some are choked out, and some trodden under feet, and the birds of the air take some away, and some have brief and brilliant life in shallow soil and quickly fade. But some grow—and out of a single word a world change comes. First a thought, carelessly said. Then an opinion used in conversation. Now a conviction lodges in the mind but you do not do anything about it. Crisis times go past and a more convenient season to live your conviction is easily arranged. Talk is easy, people say.

Then, curiously, the idea will not let you go. It begins to haunt you. You have to do something about it. Finally it becomes the dynamic of your time, energy, money, interest—your whole life's concern. Words are dangerous. They show the direction in which life moves. You can tell whether a person is a Christian by what he says.

"Let the words of my mouth, and the meditation of my heart be acceptable in Thy sight, O Lord, my strength and my redeemer."

You see I am not taking back anything I have said about the first answer. It is just a logical going on to make a second test: you can tell whether a person is a Christian—by what he does.

Now let's not think that to be a simple answer. There is more to *doing* than appears upon the surface. There is a striking illustration of William E. Hocking on what a habit is. He said, "A habit is not formed by what you do but by what you mean when you do it." Let's enlarge upon his illustration of the kite flyer: (Do not blame him for inadequacies in the illustration. It is set in my words.)

Suppose, he says, that I am going down the street to my study and I see a man in an open lot flying a kite. I stop and watch him. The next day as I go to work, I see him again and I stop once more and watch him. This keeps on for several days until apparently the man has gotten the habit each morning at that time of flying a kite—and I have the habit of watching him.

But one morning he is no longer there and I do not see him again in that field. I vaguely wonder what broke the habit. Then one day I am visiting the aeroplane factory of a friend and I see this same man bending over a table drawing lines on paper. "Who is that?" I ask. "That," my friend tells me, "is our expert on air currents."

The point you see is quite obvious. The man never got the habit of flying kites because that was really not what he was doing. What he was doing all the time was thinking about air currents, and whether he was flying a kite or drawing lines on paper, it was really doing the same thing. It was what he meant when he did it that made the habit.

Let's illustrate this further by such things as going to church or attending committee meetings. It is the why of action that is important. Do you, for example, go to committee meetings to preserve an ancient institution; to see that wheels run smoothly; to raise a budget? Or do you go to committee meetings because you seek thereby to build something of the Highway of God?

A secretary of a church organization said quite

frankly the other day in telling a small group of us why he would not take certain steps which would require leadership out ahead of his constituency. "I hold my job not by taking stands on controversial issues but by showing a numerical and financial report up to or a little better than last year."

A *little* better. What a revealing word that word "little." Not too much advance because that would make the next year's job too hard. A little better.

"That's the way I hold my job," he said.

Now, of course, he was a very wise man in the ways of this world. Because that is the test his particular constituency apparently demanded, his leadership —so-called—was a finding out what his constituency was going to do anyway and then, like a spotted coach dog running along with head proudly raised beneath the carriage, pretending that he was their leader.

Jesus pointed out very clearly in two incidents this distinction within the same action. One, you know very well. That parable about the two men who went up into the temple to pray.

The other is from the religious writings of His time which were not, for various reasons, chosen to be in the Bible when the books which comprised it were placed in the "covers." It is out of one of these apocryphal writings that we are told this incident.

Jesus came upon a man working on the Sabbath day. This was, from a literal interpretation of the religious law, a sin. But Jesus said to him: "Man, if you truly know what you are doing, you are blessed." By this He meant that if the man had a reason which was good for this apparent breaking of the law, it was right. It would then be a part of the "exceeding righteousness" of those who had seen that the Sabbath was made for the help of man and not for his hindrance. "But," Jesus went on, "If you do not know what you are doing you are accursed and a breaker of the law."

There is a church greatly excited about the number of people flowing through it. Some one is always alert to count you on a clicker when you go there. You go into the library before the service and you are counted there. You drop in on the Young People's meeting and are counted there. You go to the cafeteria for Sunday night supper and are counted there. You attend the Popular Sunday Evenings—that's the name of the service—and are counted there. You stay afterward to the pastor's forum discussion and are counted there. The statistics are hectically impressive.

But what came out? This five-times-recorded individual in that one Sunday Evening—what is he? Not how many went in but what kind of people came out is the only real test of a church, and it is not an easy test to make. It is what the church does to you that is its test. It is by what a man does with his life that you can tell if a person is a Christian.

Please do not think I am saying that that five-times-counted individual had had nothing done to him. He might very possibly have come out a new man.

Nor am I saying that those who want Christ's way should test their success by the meagerness of their following. Some people glory in being a minority and this is false thinking. The Church must succeed in the multitude. And when the multitudes pass by we hear Jeremiah wail quite properly, "Is it nothing to you, all ye that pass by?" In like manner Jesus weeps: "O Jerusalem, Jerusalem . . . and ye would not." Though Jesus knew the way to the Kingdom was through the inner circle of the Twelve, His heart was with the unheeding multitudes and he ached over the sons of men because they had eyes and did not see.

Seeing so clearly that what a man does was the only convincing test which could move the multitudes, Jesus constantly insisted: You can tell that a person —or a world—was the Father's by what was done. "Thou hast said." "This do." Religion translates life's mysteries into meanings. It transforms the lives and the life of the world.

This is the main point in Jesus' idea of the life with God. *Religion must evidence its power to transform.* To be unconformed to this world is not enough, nor to remain content while any other remains conformed to it. So long as there is one individual untouched by the transforming idea, that individual is a concrete denial to the faith of Christ. The idea of Jesus must work for all men or it is not completely true for any man.

Here was Jesus' great concern for the *one* who had gone astray. He proclaimed an idea which was for all men. There are not religious types and non-religious types. Some are moved by form and color, some by sound that is sensible and some by sound which is sensual, and some by silence which is more than absence of sound. All men are not transformed in the same way. But all men are transformable and an idea is not completely true which cannot touch saints and sons of shame with the knowledge of themselves as sons of God. And religion must show change—must do things to men and the world—or it is not credible. If it is not credible it will not affect the life of man and the world.

This great basic idea—that religion must evidence its power to transform all men—remains only a vague sound in the brain unless we see it done. Let's narrow it down to the reasons why it is so often only a fine but futile ideal. There are two obstacles you and I have to evidencing this fact: that it is what you do which makes people able to tell . . .; and there is one thing we can do about it.

Part of our impotence is our lack of faith in man's "power to become" a son of God. Here we find ourselves with our observation and our minds in fundamental disbelief. "We wish it were so," we argue with ourselves, "but, alas, all men and women are not saints, nor can they become so."

Truth, as one man said to me in troubled frustration, is an intuition. Religion in its pure sense—the apprehension of God: the awareness of His presence; and one's response to Him—is a gift to the few. If it has not been given, it cannot be gained.

Religion therefore, he went on, affects the world in two ways. It provides a body, an organization, an instrument or tool for the saints, who have religion just because they cannot help it. Then through their efforts and example it keeps the rest of us sinners-by-nature in line with a working decency so that the world we know does not become completely chaotic.

You are not unaware that the report of this man's feelings about religion expresses the state of mind of many people. Many of you are frankly discouraged because religion does not more effectively affect your lives. You know the words; you do not do the deeds. Life is kept in decency and is unconformed in spirit to the world's cruelties. It is little changed in practice, however, because you neither see what to do nor believe you can do what you may see.

The whole idea of religion clearly requires a choice at this point. The boy in the gutter and the girl of the street are saints by nature with the immediate possibility of holiness. It is because you do not really believe this about those you see—nor about yourself sometimes—that religion fails to be transforming. It is our fundamental lack of faith that makes so many people unhappy. They feel that while religion ought to do things, and can rightly be tested by what it does, nevertheless man can hardly be blamed for his failure to live the Christian way of life because "it can't be done."

A part of a man's lack of faith is because he has not seen the transformations. So long as "memory holds a seat in this distracted globe," I can never totally disbelieve in the possibilities of life's transformations. I go back to two letters which came in by the same mail. One said, "Thanks for ignoring the fool in me and believing in the good which was there but in which I did not believe myself."

And the other: "Why you believed in me in the beginning I cannot see, but that you were right in your belief I now know."

One of those was a man, and the other was a woman.

Some of you may not have had the opportunity of seeing these things and that makes you discouraged when Christianity asks you to face the "starved ignoble nature" of man's life in "the desperate valleys" of his daily existence. Admitting, as we must, the difficulty in believing without seeing, I ask you to think about the classic answer to doubt, and the only answer the outside world will heed at all. It was Jesus' reply to the followers of John, when they asked, "Are You the one who shall come?"

"Go back and tell John what you saw."

It is, of course, perfectly clear, isn't it, that life must be seen to become different if Christianity is true. The only lasting and effective test of whether a person is a Christian is by what he does. Part of the reason why we do not evidence this transformed life is that we do not really believe we can be different. And a part of that lack of faith is that our minds are practical enough to need to see some one do it before we believe in it. But some people have done it, enough to make us feel—uncomfortably—that Jesus' idea of this perfect life is not as unreasonable as it sounds.

It is, as you remember, in the convincing evidence of seeing the transformed individual that you find that curious frustration of feeble souls who did not want to change. The skepticism of the world in Jesus' day was defeated because (I quote) "Seeing the man [whom they had known from his youth to be weak and worthless] standing there whole, they could say nothing against it."

You can tell whether a man is a Christian by what he does. Jesus knew men's need for seeing it done. He came into a world without hope. Prisoners of desperation we were, shuffling along in the chain gangs of the flesh. He made men believe in man—in Himself as one of them. It sounded so reasonable when He talked about it; it looked so possible when He did it. He, that gentle strong man. He, that calm and terrible one, comes hauntingly back to those who have eyes to see and ears to hear and makes man hope again in himself and all mankind. It is by what you do, that the world tells whether you are a Christian.

Being quite honest with you in presenting the truth in Christ, I must warn you that it will do things to you. No man who gives himself to the idea of God the Father, which Christ taught and lived, can ever know what it may demand of him. Whether you have let yourself go or not so that you have felt the force of a current out of which there is no release until the rapids are run, at least in observation you know that religion does things to those who have put themselves in its way. Prodigals return, Magdalenes sin no more, Peters become rocks, the gates of hell have lost their power, men become the sons of God.

Unless you know this—that religion does things,

doing things to you whether you will it or not, changing things which seem the evil nature of man's connection with the brutes—unless you can face "the starved, ignoble nature" of the world's "desperate valleys"—"death-dark valleys, doubts without a name"—unless deep in the fiber of your being there is the resiliency of that conviction that religion does things, to try to walk the ways of the world with the idea of the Highway of God in your mind will be hell on earth for you.

But there is nothing to fear in that. Observation tells us, whether we have ever experienced it or not, that religion does things. And when you have come to know that religion does things to people and events, then your intelligence steps in with a thrilling "of course," and suddenly you see that unless religion does make a radical difference in you and your areas of life, its claims are stupid.

You can tell if a person is a Christian by what he does.

And the years are going by in which the record is being graven into the life of the world: By what you say, and by what it leads you to do, you can tell whether you are a Christian.

CHAPTER THIRTEEN

A Hard Time to Be a Christian?

Y ou noticed the question mark at the end of the topic—A Hard Time to Be a Christian? It is not a statement about a fact. As a fact I would deny it. It is *not* a hard time to be a Christian. It is in fact a comparatively easy time. But the topic asks you whether you think so. Is it a hard time to be a Christian?

We must begin with an understanding. It is a hard time to get people to join the Church. Now wait a minute. If you really make them see that being a Christian means you must have a different standard of attitudes and motivations for action from the general mind, it is not easy to flood your church roll with large numbers of people. This is not a good day for nominal Christians. Nominal Christians flourish and grow up when the edges of life are fuzzy.

But if you are one of those people who really want to be Christians, these days give you a better chance than those times when, because the meaning of Christianity was less evident, the clarity of one's thought and action was less sharp.

These are the days about which Jesus was speaking in that saying, probably as much misunderstood as any he ever spoke—"I came not to send peace, but a sword." It is absurd to think that Jesus was saying, "I urge you therefore to fight against" . . . (now put in your own fear), "with bombs and battle-ships, with poison gas and pious propaganda." Jesus was saying, "Even as the taking up of the sword in-volves a people in a cause of such life-and-death importance that it will divide families, so does My way of life demand a clear-cut choice to serve God before all other loyalties, above your chief joy." I shall want to enlarge upon this point a little later but now we want to be clear about this. We are saying to those who want to be Christians: this is not a hard time to be a Christian.

We must be sure at once that no one thinks this means that being a real Christian is ever very easy. Here is a man who makes our feelings clear by writing on "Easter Day":

> "How very hard it is to be
> A Christian! Hard for you and me,
> —Not the mere task of making real
> That duty up to its ideal,
> Effecting thus, complete and whole,
> A purpose of the human soul—
> Though that is always hard to do;
> But hard, I mean, for me and you
> To realize it, more or less,
> With even the moderate success
> Which commonly repays our strife
> To carry out the aims of life."[1]

[1]Robert Browning, "Easter Day."

Browning is sometimes difficult but that ran easily enough. He states the ground of his discouragement. If we truly mean it that we want to be brothers and make a beloved community, what is the matter with us that we fail so miserably? As Paul says: "The good that I would I do not: but the evil I would not that I do. O wretched man that I am! who shall deliver me from the body of this death?"

Thomas à Kempis in the *Imitation of Christ* speaks about the entanglement in the cares and necessities of this life and asks, "What kind of life is this against which I must struggle so long as I live!" Other things in the daily life we do easily. We make a home, we have friends, we do a job, we carry out some special project, but in this business of being a Christian: why when we think we have it and everything seems to be going well we are upset by what is really only a slight breath.

> "How very hard it is to be
> A Christian! Hard for you and me,
> *To make* even the moderate success"

which we reach in other things in the daily life.

We are not now trying to understand *why* it is so difficult to be a Christian. But we would not rightly understand our present point without being sure that we know that in saying, "It is not a hard time to be a Christian," we are speaking relatively. Compared with many other times, today is an easy time to be a Christian.

The hardest time to be a Christian is when you have much. You will have to think with keenness on that statement because when you have much it is easy to imitate the Christian virtues.

Let's take only one for an example—Generosity. It may not be anything but a careless convention requiring no sacrifice and even less thought. It is a part of the multitude-experience. You do not know why you do it except that it is the thing to do.

One of the stories of Saint Francis which keeps man's naturally complacent soul from spiritual lethargy is the one which Lawrence Housman calls "Blind Eyes." The friends of Francis claimed they loved him devotedly and he told them that before noon the next day he would prove that they did not love him at all. When they gathered according to agreement at noon in the market square, they were accosted as usual by many beggars. One in particular, blind, ragged, and very dirty, held out shaking hands to them and, in a harsh voice, whined, "In the name of sweet charity, pity the blind beggar."

They recoiled a bit from the loathsome figure, hastily throwing him a coin and moving to the other side of the square. As each one of the friends of Francis came in, he heard the wail, "In the name of sweet charity, pity the blind beggar."

When all were gathered and waiting, the clock struck noon but no Francis was in sight. As they impatiently looked about and began to rejoice in their triumph over him, they saw the blind beggar shuffling over.

Why should he come to them? He had received his alms.

But when the beggar came near he straightened up, threw back his tattered cloak, and Francis was revealed.

As they began to exclaim over the way he had fooled them, Francis sorrowfully silenced them with these words:

"That I won pittance by my lies from you, and you, and you—all that was nothing: For in your hearts you had no charity. Your giving to the beggar did but help you the easier to forget him."[2]

"Having much" puts the soul of man in jeopardy. He has acquired a taste, been raised to a standard, as he calls it, in his living. I have faced in simple honesty the fact that my nation could conceivably take from me my freedom because the officials in charge of National Defense might think my realistic Christianity was stubborn and treacherous sentimentalism. Let's not think it will be any pink tea party if I should be jailed or put in a concentration camp for my conscience' sake. Conscientious objectors to war must be sensible enough to anticipate what "Can Happen Here."

It would probably surprise you, as it did me, to know what I believe I would miss most out of my standard of living. I could give up reading books; I have a lot of them in my mind. There is a good working library in my head. I could give up hearing

[2]Lawrence Housman, "Blind Eyes," in *Little Plays of St. Francis*.

music. After all, my inner ear is tuned through memory to enough of the world's great music to buoy up my spirit through many empty nights and days. I could give up having friends about me whom I could see. My sense of community, my consciousness of spiritual fellowship is too constant to be dependent upon ear, and hand, and voices. But there is something I do every day which I would not be able to do, were I to be so unfortunate as to be jailed for my faith. And it has become a symbol to my soul as the difficulty of one who has so much being a Christian. (I purposely do not mention what that "something" is, not only because it is really not important but because it might side-track your mind from thinking about what your own small, accustomed, but really unimportant luxuries may be.)

The next hardest time to be a Christian is when you have nothing. When Abel Bonnard, the poet, wrote his all too brief prose life of Saint Francis, he observes keenly, "The tragedy of poverty is the limitation it puts upon one's charity." By that he did not mean that one lost the chance to be Lady Bountiful, or the Lord of the Manor distributing careless largess. He meant the things you and I know. No matter how much we do, if we are sensitive to the needs of the world of people, there are things we know are needed which just a bit of money would fix. And we haven't it.

Recall the moment when you were stuck. You had used up all your own money and all the sources you knew of from which you might get help. Yet here was something which needed to be done and which you wanted to do. But you had nothing.

That is what Bonnard meant. The limitation it puts inevitably upon your ability to do what you see needs to be done. This is the beginning of the difficulty of being a Christian when you have nothing.

Then it begins to pinch you. It takes away your elbow room. A man has to have elbow room to live. Having nothing takes it away. In that interesting rambling English novel by Robert Henriques, *No Arms, No Armour*, which sketches with occasionally brilliant flashes of understanding the stunted mental and emotional life of a professional soldier, Tubby suddenly understands why Watson is so crabby. "You can't be desperately poor, again and again disappointed, defenceless, subject to unfair treatment and unreasonable chance which tosses you about like sea-borne wreckage, without getting sour and weary."

One of the reasons why the Church has in spots lost its nerve these days when it should speak with clear and certain voice on the principles which time and circumstances should not change, is because the people who are for the moment the body of the Church are scared inside and do not want to show it. Then in their fear, which they are trying to conceal, they instinctively pull the horizons of their thought in close, restrict to a narrowed circle the circumference of their feelings, draw back their frontiers of action to more easily defended areas.

The fear of losing what you have is the greatest

fear. But next comes the claustrophobia of the spirit when through having nothing the walls of life seem to threaten closing in on you. Then it is hard to be a Christian. The what's-the-use reaction lays hold on the mind and chills the heart with dull dread.

It is easiest to be a Christian when you have enough to give you room to breathe but not so much that you lose the "touch of earth." This does not mean security. The spirit of man and of his institutions is not used enough to security to be able to stand too much of it. Jesus gave us a parable of warning on that: "Then he said unto his soul, Soul, thou hast much goods laid up for many years—take thine ease."

Enough does not mean "Boundless his wealth as wish could claim," as was written about "the man without a country." No, Proverbs said it wisely in these words:

"Two things have I required of thee; deny me them not before I die: Remove far from me vanity and lies: give me neither poverty nor riches; feed me with food convenient for me: Lest I be full, and deny thee, and say, Who is the Lord? or lest I be poor, and steal, and take the name of my God in vain." (Prov. 30:7,8.)

This *is* wisdom: to know what is enough.

But there is an inner place of security within that state in which it is easiest to be a Christian because you have not lost the touch of earth and yet you have room enough to breathe. When in spite of pressure you feel you are gaining in life, or are even holding

your own when common sense would say you should
be swept away, there comes an added specialized,
inner sanctuary of control over the living of the
Christian way. That is the place where the Church
is today and where you stand if you are a part of a
real Church. This place of certainty, in which it is not
hard to be a Christian, is in a day of crisis.

It is in crisis that one finds life is at its clearest.
Before the final break—when the issue is dramatically
clear, when the lines are sharply drawn in high relief,
then is the easiest time to be a Christian.

We are in such a moment of crisis now. We are
in a lull before the storm. These days are more important to the Christian Church in the witness of the
way of Christ than any which most of us have ever
known.

Then, as always happens before a crisis, coming
events cast their shadows before them. Have you ever
realized what that saying indicates? We see the shadows coming when men have turned their backs on the
light and are moving away. It is then the shadows
lengthen and we are aware of them.

There in the shadows, when men have turned their
backs, they feel the chill of something between them
and the light. How well Victor Hugo understood
this as he writes in his *Les Misérables:* "At certain
hours a profound chill falls upon the vanguard of the
human race. The multitude, fragile because of its
weight, fears adventure. The voice of the multitude
cries in justification:—I am young and in love. I am

old and wish to rest. I am the father of a family. I work. I prosper. I do good business. I have houses to let. I have money in government bonds. I am happy. I have a wife and child. Oh, I like all this, I wish to live; leave me in peace." Remember those words in these days ahead when you are tempted to be afraid that democracy depends upon your going to war. Remember those words when people say in fear that the love of Christ and God's Kingdom is in danger unless you strike with increasing blind ruthlessness at your fellow men.

The crisis with all its foreboding aspect comes like gathering storm. The chill winds of its darkness make a tightening gloom. Then certainly you know whether or not you are a Christian. You have a choice to make and you have made it. You are not first a citizen of the earth. You are on it and may love it as I do: its beauty, its music and poetry, its forms and color, its majestic nature and infinite possibilities in human life. You may be proud, as I am, of the struggle up and onward out of chaos which men call civilization. With all its crudities, we are en route to a Holy City. But suddenly you know— you are a Christian first.

Then the meaning of that quiet voice in a moment of crisis becomes a part of you. "Now is my soul troubled . . ." Of course it is. The cross was a failure in time. No use blinding your understanding to that fact. He had failed—so men would believe. ". . . And what shall I say?" Jesus asks. "Father, save me from this hour!" No, surely not. Then comes in the overtone of victory. "But for this cause came I unto this hour."

Those who see *that* will not be shaken in any day. These are not times when the spirit of man is downcast. It was for this cause that we came unto this hour. Serve God; and fear not. We know not His time. We do know that His way is sure.

> "He who would valiant be
> 'Gainst all disaster,
> Let him in constancy
> Follow the Master."

It is not a hard time to be a Christian.

CHAPTER FOURTEEN

What Are We Waiting For?

HAT are we waiting for? The answer is easy. What is it which keeps us back from the use of resources and power—the giving of life itself if need be? It is a single word: we are waiting for *Hope*. Men may live decent lives without hope. They do not live great lives. But without great lives there is no leadership. The path and price of leadership are dependent upon men and women who incarnate in themselves—who contain in their lives somehow—the living ideas of the world to which they have given substance.

"I wish I had never met you," a man once said to me in a moment of weariness. "You have given me back my hope. I was happier without it." By happier, he really meant comfortable or even contented. But, except in weary moments, and maybe even then, he knew life made a lot more sense; and was more sheer fun; and had a thrust in it, which made it worth while because hope was reasonable to him again.

When people come to see me on problems, I teach a great deal through the insight into life which the poets give. Out of poetry we can often create a symbol to which these troubled people can hold in time of pressure. And for this man, Browning's *Paracelsus* had been helpful to give him back hope. His symbol of vivid recollection was the phrase: "There is a Way." When he was stuck he would say it and go on as far as he could in the compilation of Paracelsus' hope which I had dug out and pieced together for him.

"There is a way:
'Tis hard for flesh to tread therein, imbued
With frailty—hopeless, if indulgence first
Have ripened inborn germs of sin to strength:
Wilt thou adventure for My sake and man's,
Apart from all reward?

"A prayer
For one more chance went up so earnest, so
Instinct with better light let in by death,
That life was blotted out—not so completely
But scattered wrecks enough of it remain,
Dim memories, as now, when once more seems
The goal in sight again. All which, indeed,
Is foolish, and only means—the flesh I wear,
The earth I tread, are not more clear to me
Than my belief, explained to you or no.

"I go to prove my soul!
I see my way as birds their trackless way.
I shall arrive! what time, what circuit first,
I ask not: but unless God send his hail
Or blinding fireballs, sleet or stifling snow,
In some time, his good time, I shall arrive:

"And if I stoop
Into a dark tremendous sea of cloud,
It is but for a time; I press God's lamp
Close to my breast; its splendor, soon or late,
Will pierce the gloom: I shall emerge one day."

The power of any man's life comes from the hope which will not let him desert his glimpses of perfection. To dream is not enough. That can become a sentimentalism. To have faith that God will "in His own ways occult" bring back the world at last to truth is not enough. That is sometimes pious and impotent resignation to existing evil. He must have hope —hope that what he does serves this good end in which he believes; will bring closer the victory of man over the world, the flesh, and the devil. *He must have hope.* A military genius, I have forgotten which one, but what he said was true, placed his finger on the secret. "Your enemy is defeated," he said, "when you have taken away his hope of victory."

Now, Hope, to be something more than wishful thinking, must be based on realistic convictions. Notice I did not say reasonable convictions, because that makes you think that there are logical, worldly reasons by which we prove our faith. This is not so. The faith by which men live great lives is rarely demonstrable in language. The word realistic is used in connection with convictions because we must not ignore facts or dodge difficulties.

The conviction upon which hope is based has to do with the kind of world in which we live and the nature of man who lives in it. Is this our Father's world? Are we the sons and daughters of God? we ask ourselves, but we know about these questions.

We know that to an individual there does come the experience of becoming a new creature. As suddenly as a clock ticks, or in the comparative brevity of an operation and convalescence, a new creature emerges who is a different being. A butterfly is not more different from its worm, a mind restored not more different from the imbecile the surgeon's skill saved it from continuing to be, than is the new creature from the old. Both types of time experience are put in, a tick of a clock and an operation, because life is not always changed in the same way. The old Bowery mission tales are objectively true. Harold Begbie's "Twice-born Men" in the Whitechapel district of London, who knew to an instant when they were born again, are valid. "I'm three years old next Tuesday," the gray-haired man said to me, and, knowing what he was, and what he is, I do not question. This creature *is* three years old next Tuesday. I have seen men, women, changed by a single sentence, by a phrase, by a moment of silent realization. We know that an individual can become a new creature in an instant. We know that.

But we put in the longer, tougher experience of an operation, too, because not all people are so fortunate. Here is one, a man, a woman, not struggling as Doctor Jekyll did with Mr. Hyde, but unified around a pagan ideal. There is no conflict within the personality because there is no recognition of anything but the standards by which one is living. Gwen, for example, in Ralph Connor's *The Sky Pilot*—most of you probably know that old favorite—is torn from her unity of thought and action by the unknown words of the Bible she has never seen, when the Pilot reads. She is a comparatively placid illustration of all kinds and conditions of experience in which the old habits struggle with the new ideas until, like Thomas à Kempis, we sometimes cry, "What kind of life is this in which it seems needful for me to struggle so long as I live?"

Thus it is sometimes that the long night watches, the sick body, the surgeon's knife, the weary convalescence, are not too strong a picture to represent this process by which a person becomes a new creature. But we know that an individual can become a new creature. We know that.

We believe that society can become new. This is our faith. If we believe that Christianity is only good for the individual but has no saving power for society, we are deceiving ourselves in going on, because no man liveth unto himself, and must some day choose his final standards. If the standards by which a man can live are different from those by which men can live, then the individual has no choice save a hermit's cave to retain his individual standards. A saved individual is not possible in an unredeemed society. Let us not forget that this is a major premise in the thought and action of any Christian fellowship. A saved individual is not possible in an unredeemed society. We are members one of the other. But we believe that society, too, can become new.

With this said, deliberately, with the backing of long thought, we then ask ourselves some questions as we try to go forward toward the ideal. As background for it, we look upon a story, not as familiar in these days to some as it once would have been: The story of Naaman, the leper. We are not looking at it as the hope of healing ourselves from some dread physical disease. Rather we see in it insight into a spiritual truth we are, by the nature of man's experience, inclined to neglect.

A man was a leper, divided from his fellows. Sick even of himself, he faced a hopeless end. Then from a humble source there came the unbelievable words, "You can be clean."

"I, Naaman, the leper, clean?" He hurried to his hope.

"I will do anything the prophet tells me to do," we can imagine him saying. "Anything! Nothing is too difficult, too impossible. I'll walk into a blazing fire. Nothing can be demanded of me that I will not do to be clean."

In that high emotion he hears the words, "Go and wash." It was a singularly dissatisfying sentence. He had expected to have all his resources tested by the prophet's demand. He is told to do a simple thing.

His reception of the words of the prophet are symbolic of the world's blindness—"Go and wash!"

And Naaman said, "Wash!—in that common stream? There are rivers in my own country more noble. I, who would have done anything, no matter how difficult, am told to 'Go and wash!' Let me out of here. I'm going home."

Then came the quiet voice of a young girl. "Sir, if he had bid thee do some great thing, thou wouldst have done it. Why not, then, do this which seems to you a lesser thing?"

There is no question in my mind that you, the individual reading this, would live greatly, if some great thing were demanded by the world situation. I have no question that my own people, whom I know, would face a world cataclysm with heroism. Men have faced wars before, and will again, without losing their sense of balance. A great catastrophe, a real test of persecution, brings out powers unbelievable to yourselves. Some of you down deep inside would almost welcome that the world put you to such a test. Men do—far more than the cynics scornfully believe they will—maintain, even in wartime, their honest profession that they are "through with war."

If some great thing were demanded of you, you would greatly live. But if you are waiting before you live out a Christian way of life until some great thing is demanded, you are fooling yourself.

This is not the major concern of a realistic Christian fellowship. When we get right down to the controlling motives of daily living, men do not base their actions on the belief that these great testing catastrophes will come. They believe that somehow—strikes and strife, war and rumors of war coming as they may—the world will hold together.

Now maybe it won't. Let us not live in the fool's paradise of believing that it will hold together by some beneficent providence invoked by the poet, as he says:

> "Yet I doubt not thro' the ages one increasing
> purpose runs,
> And the thoughts of men are widen'd with the
> process of the suns."[1]

"War may come to the world in two years, or five, or next spring, or the tinder box of the world may flame into civil strife before another Sunday comes." I found that sentence in some sermon notes for September 16 of 1934. Five years was the longest time I said, but before the five years were up, war did come to the world.

There is blood in many streets now, and down the pavement of your street and mine the funeral cortege of the civilization we have known may pass to the graveyard of history and its record of fallen greatness. Our eyes may see it.

How foolish we would be in these days to forget that what has happened to past eras may happen to our own.

I am not a prophet who sees the end and proclaims its doom. All I am doing is interpreting what we do think. We may die tonight. We may be a city sacked before another decade. The year 2000 may find our civilization as dead as Babylon or ancient Egypt—our city as ruined as Sodom and Gomorrah. We may—but we do not believe it. We do not act that way, you

[1]Alfred Tennyson, "Locksley Hall."

and I. Whatever great thing may be demanded of us, I do not know. But I do know that you and I are living, and believe we shall continue to live, in the realm of little demands. "Go and wash!"

Let us be honest, then, with our present situation and our immediate problem. We are concerned with what Christianity means to us in the commonplace.

Let's take an example of our dead hope. What makes you afraid, some of you, when you hear people say that the profit motive must be taken out of civilization? If we were not Christians, we might accent, as so many do, the adjective in that phrase. Profit! "The world cannot get along without profit," men say. Nothing in the phrase profit motive says it can. It is descriptive of motive, you see. You might say "good" motive or "bad" motive or "secondary" motive. In this case we say "profit" motive. It does not say take the profit out of society. It says take the motive of profit out as the drive and purpose of your life. You may still have to have profit to live by as society goes on, but you do not live and move and have your being because of the motive of profit. You live by the hope of the beloved community which Jesus called the Kingdom of God.

Or do you? That is, of course, the question. Do you have that hope in the fundamental decency of men and goodness of society?

The fear that comes to some people when they hear the profit motive questioned is a revelation of where they put their trust. They have no real hope save in the power of their possessions.

Now as then, the light which is the Christ can do nothing for them who are without faith, who do not believe with hope in this common daily life in which He lived and taught men to live.

What are we waiting for? The hope which makes it worth while to remain undiscouraged in daily living. I wish true leadership were dramatic. It rarely is. It is sticking to it through the common days because of the hope which will not die.

If only we could see, with our feelings as well as with our minds, that our fathers only seemed to have a greater simplicity, a more dramatic simplicity as they stood for Christ's way in their day. If we say, as sometimes we do, that life today has not, as our fathers' had, some simple issue possessing dramatic quality, we must remember it was not simple to them either. Slavery seems a simple issue to us. For them it was all mixed up with economics and politics, and social customs and the conservative conventions of daily life.

When you are in a changing moment of history, there are no clear-cut lines to draw. There is no frontier we can defend against some obvious enemy. And if you were expecting some simple answer to the questions which this book raises, you will be and must ever be disappointed. We are yeast, we are salt, we are light. And our hope is in this: that man can become a new creature; that a new earth is possible. We know it because we have seen certain individuals show us how life can be lived; we have seen changes come in social structure; and we believe that in the

ferment which is the world of today there are discoverable and attainable the knowledge and the power
to build the New Earth.

No great thing will be demanded. You must begin
to be that different creative being you are in possibility so that, tested now on simple common things
such as unwavering Christlike attitudes in a world
afraid and hopeless, you may be ready to grasp a great
demand when some day does bring it. The opportunity may pass by almost unnoticed unless you are
prepared to hold on to it.

No one can tell you what to do. That is one thing
not given to us. We can tell you how others lived.
They achieved leadership because to

> "the last giddy hour
> Of dead endurance, from the slippery, steep
> And narrow verge of craglike agony . . ."

they suffered

> ". . . woes which Hope thinks infinite;
> To defy Power, which seems omnipotent;
> To love, and bear; to hope till Hope creates
> From its own wreck the thing it contemplates;
> Neither to change, nor falter, nor repent;
> This like Thy glory, *God*, is to be
> Good, great and joyous, beautiful and free;
> This is alone, Life, Joy, Empire, and Victory."[2]

Men want to live out, and the world is waiting for,
the hope which never deserts our glimpses of perfection.

[2]Percy Bysshe Shelley, "Prometheus Unbound."

CHAPTER FIFTEEN

The Law of Eminent Domain

HAT after all should happen to the people who read this book? They should know that a man or an institution moves only so fast as the conviction he has about the loyalty which comes first; plus the ability of that man or institution to get others to see and accept it.

"What I cannot understand," said Giollet, the soldier in Jules Romain's *Verdun*, "is why it is that when they mobilized us, none of our women lay down on the tracks and cried, 'If you take our sons and husbands, it will be over our dead bodies."

"But it would not do any good. They would just be picked up and the troop trains would run a bit behind schedule because of it," was the objection of his lieutenant. "If millions of men on both sides should refuse to get mixed up in this universal crime—" the sentence did not need finishing. "But just a sprinkling of people here and there . . . you think it makes a difference however small?" Thus we would paraphrase his comment.[1]

"In the absence of those millions," was the reply, "it is still worth while to give one's mite to the cause

[1]Page 357.

of saving, if only symbolically, the dignity of man which he (by his act) plants in the invisible seed-ground of the future."

You will be always stuck unless you believe in this ultimate loyalty. It is because we are confused on this that we find we are so often impotent. You know the feeling from observing life about you. You are divided, torn by conflicting emotions, possessed of devils because you do not feel strongly enough that there is a cause which is greater than your personal rights or the possessions and privileges of any persons. Civilization rises or falls, progress exists or life stagnates because of the accent people place on where authority lies, on what loyalty is.

There is a principle of living which we should lay upon our spirits. We call it in law the right of eminent domain. It is to ordinary life what a public emergency is to times of catastrophe. Let's start with catastrophe. That is easier to see.

"No one has a right to burn down my house," is a statement which sounds reasonable. But it is not true. There are quite a few circumstances when strange people have a right to burn it down or blow it up or use it for other purposes. A fire is sweeping over a city. Your house stands in the way. It may be a menace as a possible conductor of fire or may be needed as a fire break. Public emergency does not consider your rights in that moment. This is an accepted principle of society. The laws of man are one with God's laws of humanity in this matter.

The Right of Eminent Domain is not the same law

but it is similar. No emergency is involved but the interest of the public is again the superior authority. The Right of Eminent Domain is the right to change things as they are on this earth for the public good.

One needs only to think as he drives along a road to see this principle in its success and failure. Look next time you take a long drive at the curves, the dangerous and constantly more dangerous curves, of our modern highways. Why is that S curve there? The road should go across that field but it turns half-left and winds around a farm, runs dangerously close to a schoolyard, ducks up and down and up again over little hills, joins the direct line of the road by another curve, this time a sharp one.

Why does it do such criminally dangerous things? Because that farmer's influence was too strong with the selectmen. He did not want the highway to cut across his best field, and interfere in addition with the way his house was set. And so the highway, now laid in concrete, makes an ugly S curve where it has always been since horse and buggy days. That curve in my mind is up in New Hampshire.

As you come off the bridge across the Connecticut at Northfield, there is a different story written by the road for all who ride to see. There once was a right-angle turn to the left there and then a sharp hairpin around a bump of a hill. On that curve a house and a gas station; on the hill a house with a view over the river. The way lay through the hill quite obviously, straight and level. The man on the curve did not want it to be made where it belonged. It would destroy his gas business; it would leave his house off on a loop which would be little used and allowed to fall into decay. The man on the hill did not want the road to go where it belonged. It made his house unliveable, destroyed his view, made an ugly cut right through a spot sentimentally and æsthetically dear to him. But the road belonged there and they put it there. By Right of Eminent Domain, for the good of the commonwealth, to serve the need of the whole—they put it there. Straight ahead you drive now off that bridge into a cut with its steep sides reminders only of the obstacle of a hill which had stood in the way. Straight and safe the highway now runs.

If they had waited to get the consent of the two men, they would be waiting yet. But there is a principle, of which road building is a specific example, which is inherent in both the logic and the practice of society: by Right of Eminent Domain no special privilege or private interest can be allowed to stand in the way of the good of the whole.

You see that plainly when men make a path upon the earth to bear the traffic of the world. The price is plainly marked: you must hew to the line and let special privilege or personal desires fall where they may. We know that men can abuse the Right of Eminent Domain and turn it to dishonest ends. But the principle we believe; its practice we must defend. There is no leadership of men or institutions without that right of making a way straight and sure to the desired and destined end.

But having illustrated from the marks men make

upon the earth which form the plain path here in time, let us now see it work in the life of man. How does this principle work in what he does with his existence, in the far less easy to see responsibility man has toward the City of God and the way that leads to it?

Is there in your conception of your life a right of eminent domain which lets no fear for self make your spirit timid or your hold on the right weak? It is only those who feel what Whitman called "The potent, felt, interior command, a message from the heavens whispering to you even in sleep," who get "the urge, the ardor, the unconquerable will" to face this world without cringing.

We should take a tough example since we are using only one to illustrate. The opportunities to illumine this point are so many in life and it was not easy to select one only.

It may seem queer to take an example which ended in what men call failure—because the child died. They did not save her after all. But if I had taken a success, then any one could follow. And while this book is addressed to every one, it is not talking about just any one. It is aimed at you who might be a leader. The leader has to see the ultimate good. Any earth-blind man can set up a camp in the wilderness and pick up daily bread. It takes more than any one of us can deliver alone to bring the people of the earth to the Promised Land at last.

Come back with me then to a true story which some of you may have seen in the papers. It was a paragraph of news on that day it happened. Alfred Noyes called the incident "The Last Voyage" in his trilogy *The Torch Bearers*. It was an emergency operation on board ship—which is one of the recurrent dramas of the seas. He made it the protonic center of his conviction that man's job is to bear the torch as well as he can and not demand the pay of success in time for his service.

The great ship pounds through the storm. A child lies desperately ill of a rare disease. Only a skillful operation can save her and the ship's doctor knows what skill and techniques he needs and knows also that he does not have control over either. "If only I could consult Marlowe of Johns Hopkins," he sighs.

"Marlowe?" says a startled voice. "Why he's on the *City of Paris* only four hundred miles away. I saw his name in the ship's news this noon."

Quickly the radio stutters out its message. It seems stuttering to us although it is as exact as a mathematical formula. Dot-dash, dot-dot-dash, dot-dash-dash-dot. The tense room seems filled with vibrant signals. The brain of Marlowe, four hundred miles away, receives the diagnosis through the dark, over the turbulent waves. He prescribes, directs the technique of the operation, stands by to help in consultation as the operation proceeds. The great ship idles down to scarcely perceptible motion.

The paraphernalia of an operation, anæsthetic, sterilization, and so forth, are prepared. In Noyes' presentation a tall figure, presumably the observing poet, stands outside the door.

An anxious voice inquires, "Can they save her?" "Yes," he replies. "They can. But who are they?"

He answers his own question in his mind as he paces the deserted decks. He sees the card games going on in the lounge; hears their gay unthinking mirth. Not there!

He strides in imagination the corridors of history and peeks into many cubicles of space where men have lived their span of time. He sees the whole power of man's long search to know, his struggle to have power to control the forces which would destroy him, converging on that cabin as, a speck only on the mighty ocean and seemingly there alone, that doctor does his best to save that life.

There was a doctor once who turned down what the conventional world calls success and went out

> "Into that dark, that blind, that crooked street
> Called by the crowd Obscurity,"

because "he had a tryst with truth." In that tryst he found what is now a commonplace of knowledge for all doctors and now gave this doctor a chance. France, Germany, Holland, a Swedish scientist and a Swiss maker of instruments of precision, an American organization, an Italian inventor, all assist that seemingly lonely figure. They speak to his brain, hand him instruments, give him formulæ, and all the while through the dot-dash of an electrical impulse, sent out into the dark and answered from the dark, the brain of Marlowe guides his hand. Alone in that cabin one man does his best. But *they* are there.

These are they who have been touched by the divine imperative, the Law of Eminent Domain in the spirit-land of man. "Unconsciously, and even against his will," man has heard the

> ". . . strange imperative whisper far within
> Affirm, Thou must, despite thine own desires
> —(thou must)
> Though all *thy* hopes be shattered by this choice
> Thou *must* uphold the right; and in thy power
> To hear this absolute whisper and defy
> What seems the wheel of Nature, thou hast
> proved . . .
> To thine own true self . . . and in the king-
> doms of reality beyond
> This world of fleeting shadows . . .
> Though blind men cannot see, or deaf men hear,
> The three great affirmations which alone
> Can save mankind from utter chaos now,
> God, Freedom, Immortality."[2]

"I am the way, the truth, and the life."

This world will never be the Kingdom of God until we know that we were called by Him to take up our own cross and, for the joy set before us, endure its suffering and its seeming failures, or any other thing it means, as we tear down and plow through and build that Highway for our God.

There on that Way, at the very limit of our strength to carry it, we plant that cross which is ours so that, over its outstretched arms, those who walk with us

[2]Alfred Noyes, "The Last Voyage," pp. 139–40. Frederick A. Stokes Company.

and who follow after may see the way plain. That cross points back over a way made straight, and before us through the world's glib impossibles, stretching an imperative line which, by right of eminent domain, we must push on without fear until we come unto the City of God.

Let me say again that a man or an institution moves only so fast as his conviction about his first loyalty will let him. And the world will see this and accept it only when it sees that we mean it out beyond failure or the tests of time. There is a Right of Eminent Domain for the Children of God.

CHAPTER SIXTEEN

Squatter Sovereignty

"HIS is mine" was heard in the caves of the earth before the dawn of history. Low and high it has endured down recorded time. Dog in the manger growling over a bone he could not use, or father rejoicing "This my son was lost and is found," evidence the hold possession has on the life of men. "To have and to hold, from this day forward . . . till death do us part" says the marriage ceremony. Mankind has a keen sense of things that belong to him.

We must go back to an historic principle called Squatter Sovereignty, and to a legal procedure about possessions from which this historic practice comes. Let me merely give you the material, supplying the history and the illustrations. You apply it to yourself wherever it may fit, making your own moral judgments.

Let's begin it with an experience common to us all—that known as the Right of Way across property. When an individual or a group of people have passed back and forth across a tract of land until by custom that way is established, there is acquired by that individual or group and the public they represent, a right of way. You are always bumping up against it in this life.

I met it first as a small boy playing football on a vacant lot. The policeman said, "Beat it, kids, you can't play here today." He gave no explanation, only orders, but a wise father told me that the owner was closing the property off from the public for a day, lest a right of way be established.

Next I met it in Birmingham, England, where one side of a railroad station was closed for twenty-four hours so that it could be established that the company had disputed once a year the right of the public to pass through the property from one street to another.

New Yorkers meet the principle once a year in the summer time when they try to cross a street in Rockefeller Center. Chained off and guarded from accustomed feet is a little strip of pavement which might by law be lost to private control if the right of passage through it were not disputed once a year. This is the legal principle of the Right of Way.

There is a second similar type of experience in which the so-called squatter acquires rights. This is a part of the history of the settlement of our country. Vast tracts of lands were given, by the King originally and by the government of the colonies eventually, in the great unknown West. They were given by drawing lines upon a map. The lands were ample to cover unknown difficulties such as the presence of large lakes or mountain ranges which were unfit for habitation or cultivation. "Oh, take another inch on the map," was easy to say.

These lands were not occupied by the people to whom they were given and, as time went on, the flood of westward-moving new settlers came to these lands. They settled there. They used the lands. They cleared the forests and cultivated the fields. They established their communities and developed the territory.

Belatedly, the people to whom the land had been granted woke up to the fact that there was value here. "Get off my land," they said.

With established communities in the unknown territory, the colonies, afterward states, began to say, "Look here, you are a part of our domain."

Take a quick look at the maps of those days. Massachusetts went out through Buffalo and included the as yet undiscovered Niagara Falls; the State University at Madison, Wisconsin, would also, in her claims then, still belong to Massachusetts. Connecticut extended to the Mississippi River and, according to her claims then, Chicago would now be in the State of Connecticut. Virginia not only took in everything to the west up to the Big River, including Kentucky, most of Indiana, Ohio, and Illinois, but claimed as well Wisconsin and Minnesota. Technically, according to deeds or grants, the contentions of the individual or government were correct.

But—the squatter had to be considered. This was no shiftless irresponsible claimant to rights. He had discovered, developed, settled, and was using the land. And there grew up the principle of Squatter Sovereignty. It was not opposed to a principle of English law on which our own laws are largely based. The principle of Right of Way established by continuous public use we know. There was another principle called the principle of Adverse Possession. Periodically you will read in the papers about a suit of descendants of the early Dutch to recover their right to the land on which Columbia, for example, stands. You do not need to feel concerned. No great-great-great-great-grandchild of some old Dutch farmer is going to evict Nicholas Murray Butler from his domain. Even though the contention might be right (it usually proves to be false as a matter of fact), the principle of Adverse Possession would protect those who have developed Columbia.

The principle could be stated this way: they possessed the land because for a period of time they lived on it, and no one told them it was not theirs. After a while they could not be driven off.

Out of such reasonable good sense there grew the principle of Squatter Sovereignty. The squatter had two principles. These were principles in a spiritual sense for him; they were principles in a legal sense against the claims of others. The principles were these:

A man has a right to the land on which he has settled. He must use the land he claims.

This meant that no absentee owner, be he the King himself, had the right to throw settlers off land they had won from the wilderness. But no man had a right to hold land which he did not use.

So far, it sounds as if we were conducting a class in history or law. Let's turn to some familiar stories:

"And Jesus went up into the temple of God and cast out them that sold and bought in the temple and overthrew the tables of the money changers and the seats of them that sold doves. And He said unto them, 'It is written, My house shall be called the house of prayer, but ye have made it a den of thieves.'"

It was one of the scandals of the day, the commercializing of the custom of sacrificing. It was a day when prayers were made with sheep and doves instead of with words or candles. But the sale of the birds and beasts for sacrifice had become a racket. Not just any dove would do. It must be one passed by the board of censors. Therefore a monopoly of the temple traders grew up and they gradually penetrated further and further into the temple precincts until "the house of prayer had become a den of thieves." It was squatter sovereignty on their part. The temple did not object when they came in. Finally they objected when it was suggested that they go out. They believed they had established a right. And because the temple was not being used by those who should have used it, the money changers returned to the temple even after being thrown out (or so I've heard).

Again, we see a man who was possessed of a devil. Don't worry about the shape of the devil. Whatever skepticism you may have on his personality there is no skepticism possible on the primary fact of "a man possessed." Evil dwelt in him. He *was* possessed. Then from that man, through the expulsive power of a new and beautiful and clean idea, the devil—oh, take off the "d" if you prefer—the evil *was* thrust out.

The devil in the story recognized a fact when he saw it. Here was a superior force, a prior right. He departed and departed fast. He believed the good idea when it said, "You do not belong here. This man belongs to me. This is my dwelling place." But the principle of the right of possession which the squatter had applies. Man has a right to the land he settles but no right to hold that which he does not use.

Two of Galsworthy's young people, discussing life, make this comment about truth which older people have advised them not to try to apply now.

"But truth gets tired of waiting too long, and one day, when you're not expecting it, comes up and says: 'Now choose—it's your only chance. Are you going to use me or not? If not, I'm going.' How awful, the other replied, if one didn't realize the moment was there, and missed it."

It happened thus with the man in Jesus' story. He thought he was all right because he had expelled evil. But he did not use life for good. And the devil found this out and gathered seven other spirits more deadly than himself and came back and asserted his squatter's rights. You have a right to what you occupy. You have no right to hold that which you do not use.

Here is where Abraham, in the ancient story of a man going out into the wilderness with what he believed, differs from the man in the parable of Jesus who was afraid to use his talent. Here is where we are so often like him. To which him do I refer? That is your answer to make.

We have a right to a great tradition in the Church

today. And there are two ways to try to preserve its great truth. You can make of God's truth a monument. Beautiful in form, lovely to look at, the present can make of the past tradition exhibits for a museum. Under lock and key the record of a vanished glory can be preserved. Watched and guarded, the form of greatness can be retained. That is one way to preserve a great truth; to make it a record in a museum.

There is another way; to make truth a movement; not to look back with longing eyes on the land from whence you came out—as Robinson calls it "the grim, nostalgic passion for the great that once was theirs." The man who felt that had known easy days and success beyond that of most people in the world and now with dark days about him he crouched in his familiar place: "Fearing to think, secure only so long as he lay motionless." Thus do men in days of flux shudder and shiver. If only I could be sure of what might happen, they wail, I would move again, but I was afraid and went and digged in the earth and hid what I had lest I lose it. And he did lose it.

It is true of more than gold. It is true of life, of spirit, of truth itself. There is a squatter sovereignty over life. It must be used to be your own. Goethe, the German poet, once said about wealth (and he meant of all kinds), "What you have inherited from your fathers you must first earn for yourself before you can call it yours."

You were to make the moral judgments. I must keep faith with you on that. But it seems fair to suggest two essential reactions to the world we live in.

We have an as yet unoccupied territory of the spirit to keep in our own hands and the only way to keep it from going by adverse possession into the permanent keeping of evil is to assert first of all our own rights of possession. "This is mine," we say over life and time, over the world and the flesh— This is mine!

We have come closer to losing our right over life than we may think. The forces of doubt and despair, of enmity and evil, have established a nine-points possession over the common life.

There is one thing we must not neglect to remember about Adverse Possessions, however. If not too long delayed, one can reassert a right of possession even over long-established squatter's use. Even though nine points of the law are apparently against you and the forces of evil squat determinedly on the life they have long occupied, a determined and confident assertion of prior claim can evict this bumptious squatter.

Nobody ever stated this better than Carlyle in his tale of the Wanderer in *Sartor Resartus*, who walked the barren and unexplored surface of the earth appalled by the hold that the wilderness and the desert had over that which was, in some men's lives, a garden spot of beauty. And the Wanderer called over the desert and through the wilderness and into the cave of the winds, "Why, why?" and received no answer. No answer until the devil felt that man was licked and gloatingly said, "Poor deluded fool, dost thou not know that thou art fatherless and outcast and the universe is mine?" To which the Wanderer made reply,

"I am not thine but free and forever hate thee." We must first establish the fact that we dispute the right of way over life, of this evil which seems to possess the earth.

The other reaction is not as easy to judge. But we must remember that we have no right to that which we do not use. This is the second principle of Squatter Sovereignty. When I came back from the mud of the trenches to a world which had a chance to become new, I saw and still see in the Church the greatest force to possess the earth for good that I know. I went into it then not knowing whether the Church would receive a passion which burns even more fiercely now than it did then. My greatest concern through these years is not that people who are blind do not see; but that people who say they see will not go through the processes of remaining in the Church and cultivating this land of our promise.

This is the precious possession of the fellowship of Christ's way which we almost lost. It will take a determined assertion of right and a constant occupancy to reclaim it. Pioneer settlement is not easy. No wonder some people want to go back to the fleshpots of Egypt or, captured by Babylon, forget the glory of the Holy City. But if men and women who see the need of this world would only *not* give up the Church, they would *yet* build on the earth we dwell on, a common life worthy of our God. There is a Squatter's Sovereignty over life. No evil could possess it, if we used it as we could.

CHAPTER SEVENTEEN

The Door We Had Forgotten

IT IS stupid to pretend that there is always a way, if we can find it, to work out every desire of life. An individual often comes to the place where there is no open door by which he can escape from his imprisonment in time, or through which he can go to gain what he may want for himself. Good things, too, these may be and needed if he is to live.

A farmer in the Dust Bowl. It is not enough to use Voltaire's placid-sounding sentence, "We must cultivate our gardens." Try cultivating your garden while the dust storm blots out the sun and makes the rivers run bottom up and buries the top soil in drifts of sterile dust. He cannot stay and live, and there is no place to go. In that moment, as an individual, he has only the bitter taste of The Grapes of Wrath to sustain a life which is doomed—doomed so far as his power, alone and unassisted, to gain bread for himself and those he loves.

A black man in a white world. "Lord, being dark," he cries, "forewilled to that despair my color shrouds me in, I strangle in this yoke drawn tighter than the worth of bearing it. Too great a price this birth entails just to be man." If, then, a black man just wants to live as so many white men can live, he is fooling himself. There are times when, for what some call living, there are no open doors for him. Not yet can a black man be just a man—taken for what he is. Not yet in this Christian civilization as we call it. The black man, as an individual, wanting normal decent things which are natural to want, is smothered in the clinging folds of "color" which make a "shroud" about him.

A Christian in a world at war. He is stupid if he thinks he can live in isolated security from the world. He should not expect to be able to keep his freedom of opinion and keep his job, and be secure himself in a world gone mad because of its insecurity. For him as an individual this is not possible. He may have no open door at all to save himself. He may have to endure the stupid brutalities of men whose nerves are on edge and who take it out on him for refusing to be a part of what we may feel with an awful sense of doom is an inevitable stupidity. He cannot live in any way as a part of the world because every part of it is a party to the sin of war. And yet he cannot die. He is caught in a moment when for him as an individual, interested in himself (note the qualifying phrase—as an individual interested in himself), there is no open door for him.

A woman in a man's world. A part of the peculiar gentleness of Jesus with all women was an intuitive understanding of the tragedy of so many women's lives. He knew that the sharp bitterness, acid in its action, which came from the lips and showed in the attitude of many a vixen, was from the feeling that she was in the straitjacket of the history and the psychology of the mind of men who dominated the world. You can dress the fact up in the pretty fairy tale of the Sleeping Beauty but you do not get away from the fact that in a man's world the individual woman, if she is concentrated primarily about the very natural concerns of self, finds herself so often with no open door.

You might wish—as I do—that it were not so. That the farmer in the Dust Bowl could cultivate his garden; that the black man could be quite simply just a man; that a Christian could be a little candle of brightness in a dark and windy world; that a woman could forget that she has to live in a man's world. But there is no use kidding yourself. There are times when the individual is caught in forces outside his control.

Yet we ordinary people sometimes forget in our self-concern something the saints have always known: there is always a way open for a man to serve God. It is the door we had forgotten.

There was a psychological experiment which received considerable publicity not long ago in which a rat was placed in a cage with many doors. Behind one—one only—there was food and freedom. The others led to nothing. Upon that door they placed a mark. The rat learned that the mark meant food and freedom. Then after a year they put the mark on a door that was locked and the rat went mad trying to go through where there was no way.

The title of this chapter refers to that experiment and the way Maxwell Anderson used it in his play *Key Largo*, which has one of the most moving curtain lines I have ever heard. Because I want to have you feel, if I can, an emotion about that line which made me walk the streets for a long while, trying to keep back the tears, I shall hold back the line until we have built its atmosphere.

Poor, desperate, frightened, hopeless world! We dare not believe there is a way. We knew it once, but we have forgotten. The topic refers to that. But beyond the experiment and the play's use of it, it refers to an experience which is recurrent for so many men throughout the ages. Men forget there is always a way for a man to serve God.

It is not a very reasonable way as men reckon reason. When Joan of Arc knew she was to be burned she did what many martyrs in the past have done, recanted. It was but for a moment and then she was firm again, but in that moment, which she shares with many great men and women, she says the reasonable word. "It is not commonsense to walk into a fire."

No, it is not commonsense. It is not commonsense to go to Jerusalem, whatever your Jerusalem may be, when your enemies are waiting for you there. It is not commonsense to let your disciples go unstopped from you to the priests of the established order who seek to destroy you. It is not commonsense to refuse the help of the sword when your own life is at stake. It is not commonsense to care only about God. Jesus' idea of what is reasonable is not the same as that of the world.

But to say it is not reasonable as the world judges is not to say that there is no way. There is a door for those who dare to use it, by which it is always possible to serve God.

Jesus never said His way was easy, but He always said it was not impossible; that any man, which means every man, could do it if he only would.

A part of our not doing it is man's natural lack of faith in what he is. We wish it were so, that we too had the nature of the saints, but alas, we say—sadly or in relief as the mood may hit us—all men and women are not saints; nor can they become so. Really to see God, as one man once put it to me in an argument which I shall probably always remember—really to see God is an intuition, not an achievement. He spoke in troubled frustration because he wanted more than anything else to believe what he rightly thought I believed. Religion in its pure sense, he said, and by that I mean the apprehension of God—the awareness of His presence and one's response to Him—is a gift to the few. If it has not been given it cannot be gained.

The Church, therefore, he went on, affects the world in two ways. It provides first a body, an organization, an instrument or tool for the saints—who have religion just because they cannot help it. Then through their efforts and example it keeps the sinners in line with a working decency so that the world we know seldom gets completely chaotic. But the saints who see God are forever different from the rest of us who never can see God since we have not been given the gift.

I am not unaware that he expresses the state of mind of many of you. Concealed behind the conventions of an Easter crowd, for example, for all its appearance of a clothes' parade, there is probably more wistful longing for, but fundamental unbelief in, the reasonableness of Christ's way than in all the rest of the Sundays of the year. Frankly you are discouraged because religion does not more effectively affect your lives, which are normally decent and, deep down, unconformed to the world's obvious cruelties, yet in practice are changed so little and are so little different from the world about you. You neither see what to do nor believe, if you should catch a glimpse of it, that you can do what you may see.

Here is where you must realize that the idea of Jesus crosses sharply with the sincere ideas of the man who was talking with me.

Quite clearly and without exception Jesus states a fundamental mental decision here. Jesus would have you remember that the least probable people have evidenced this possibility of Holiness and so long as memory persists any one who has seen this transformation of a sinner to a saint can never totally disbelieve His ordinarily unreasonable idea.

With Francis of Assisi in the world of experience we cannot totally disbelieve even in the de Medicis. Judas is not the ultimate in life when Peter wobbles at last to his place as the rock upon which the Church can be built. And no devil-possessed man or woman need feel forever lost in the abandoned graveyards of the world while the maniac of Gadara and Mary of Magdala are the companions of Christ's Way. He took these people who had no chance, who were outcasts from the normal world and who did not believe in themselves, and showed them there was a door into life which they had forgotten was there. This was a miracle in itself—a miracle of nature which is far more difficult to believe than the miracles of the supernatural.

If you want a minor miracle, go to those churches where a man waves his hands and recites some ancient formulæ of words to make Christ's presence real. There is a uniqueness therein of a miracle apart from nature and it is not hard to believe if you believe first of all in an all-powerful and capricious God.

The major miracle of Christianity is to be found in those churches where He whose name we bear took this common stuff of nature, which we are, and made us see what a man can do with his soul as he transforms this body, mind, and spirit with the miracle of God's presence.

The greatest miracle of all, maybe, is when He takes a man who has lost his ideals and has learned to crawl like a worm that he may live himself no matter at what cost to others, and makes that man remember a way to live he had forgotten because he was afraid to die.

Such a man was King McCleod in Anderson's play. Here is victory—that strange unreasonable victory of life triumphant because it is not afraid to fail or die, and which thinks not of itself in the end.

There were in Spain some American boys of the Lincoln Brigade. They were there because they wanted to help the underdog and felt it was the last stand of democracy against the forces which would destroy decency. It does not matter at the moment whether they were right. They thought they were. But their cause is lost—definitely lost. King McCleod of the big ideas runs to save his life, and when he is caught, turns to fight with Franco's troops against his erstwhile cause. He did it to live and finds it is not living.

In trying to restore his confidence in himself as a man, when the war is over he goes to the relatives of the boys he had led to Spain and had deserted. They had stayed because they believed there was something in the world that would rather die than accept injustice. But all the relatives turned from him in disgust until down in Key Largo in Florida, d'Alcala, the blind father of Victor, his special friend, and d'Alcala's daughter Alegre, forgive him.

There King McCleod finds himself again in danger, for the gangsters, also there, are a danger to d'Alcala's daughter. Thinking to save her without endangering himself, McCleod tells the gangsters he is d'Alcala's son and Alegre is his sister. It is a futile lie anyway as he soon finds out. Not only can he not get away with it with the gangsters, but d'Alcala will not accept his lie because it is taking the easy way.

Then the plot closes in. There has been a murder

by the gangsters which the sheriff must pin on some one. It is either McCleod or two Indians down by the shore who had escaped from a road gang. Since some one must take it the Indians will do. It is Mc-Cleod's life against two Indians, he has never seen, and he lets the innocent bear the blame.

Then they bring them in.

> "Two Indians," he says, "I thought, let them die
> It won't matter. But now I see their faces
> I can't let them die *for me*."

Knowing that he is dooming himself to death, King McCleod maneuvers the head gangster into a position where it is a test of nerves whether or not the gangster will shoot. The gangster breaks, and in shooting makes the gun in King's hand go off in the stomach of Murillo, the real murderer.

King is, of course, mortally wounded too and drops back against the table. Painfully he raises himself upon one elbow and speaks:

> "Once in a thousand years a mortal man
> gets the same chance twice," he says,

and you remember how he has spoken about running from the "storm" in Spain only to be driven down to this Key to choose again. But now he has learned, what he had earlier denied, that "a man must die for what he believes." "Strangely enough," he adds, "I'm not afraid to die."

> ". . . there was another door,
> and one I never leaped at, and there's food

for the soul and mental sustenance, and mirth
  . . . no, let me alone.
Let me sit up and look him [death] in the face
Whoever he is."

There was a door he had forgotten, and through
that door his life slips out in victory.

They stood there tense at first—the sheriff, and the
daughter who is safe, and the blind man whose son
had died in Spain. The blind man fixed, as blind men
listen immovable when motion is going on about
them, hears the sheriff speak:

"You can't be sorry
  for a man that planned it, and it all worked out,
  and he got what he wanted."

Then suddenly the sheriff realized that the murder
case is now washed up. He can mark it solved and
closed. Murillo, the gangster, is dead and the law has
no unfinished business. But as he lets go his tension
and is about to go away, he turns to d'Alcala, the
blind father, standing there so rigidly.

"Just for the record—sir," he asks the question,
"This *was* your son?" Quietly the blind man answers,
"He was my son."[1]

It is now no lie. McCleod may have done many
wrong things including the dramatic violence of the
end. That is not the present point. He had come unto
himself in forgetting himself and had earned the right
to be true son of d'Alcala's spirit.

[1]Maxwell Anderson, *Key Largo*, pp. 122 ff. Anderson House.

There is a quiet pride in any father's heart when he can say those words. "This is My beloved Son in whom I am well pleased" was the phrasing of that revelation of the mind of God when Jesus began His ministry of life.

And Jesus always told us: You are not defeated if you will pay the price. It is not easy but it is not impossible for you. Remember the words of Isaiah. "I will bring the blind by a way they knew not." Remember my promise to you, said the Good Shepherd who will give His own life for His sheep. "I am the door, by Me if any man enter in he shall be saved."

In the bright inner light of a hope renewed and life reconsecrated, be silent for a moment as you ask yourself, "Is there a door to serve God which I had forgotten?"

There is light enough to see The Way. A Candle in the Wind is not enough to light this world. But the Light which the world still needs can be made flesh. He showed us that and told us we could do it too.

CHAPTER EIGHTEEN

The Great Day of Creation

PEAKING as a man on the street rather than as a philosopher, the great day in creation was the fourth day, not the first. "In the beginning," begins Genesis, "the earth was without form and void, and darkness was upon the face of the deep . . . and God said, 'Let there be light,' and there was light."

What a moment! For the first time the mole-blind earth saw what it was. The writer of Genesis calls it a day when light was created. Who can blame him? The mind of man had to rest anyway, whatever God had to do, when that one thing was done. Think of it! There was only darkness all-pervading, impenetrable. Then suddenly there was light and forever afterward darkness was defeated. It had met its master. "The darkness has never been able to comprehend it," says John, and the word comprehend really means to overcome, to blot it out, to be superior to it.

I do not blame the writer of Genesis for calling it a day. There are a lot of things I can take in my stride. When a lawyer called me up one day and said that the church had been left a legacy of over one-half a million, I said that was good news, would he write me a letter giving the details, and I turned at once to my next appointment. Believe it or not, that is one of the things you can take in your stride.

The thing that stops me is to see a soul take fire, catch the radiance, become illumined. I am not much good the rest of that day. Life has suddenly overflowed its capacity. Sometimes you have to go through the motions but you cannot take them in. Life is too full. Some one who walked in darkness has seen a great light. That is a quotation from the Bible, in case you did not see the label on it. The account goes on: "They that dwelt in the shadow of death, upon them hath the light shined."

What makes that experience so wonderful is that "you've got something there" which has licked the darkness. There is a one-way arrow on this. You never hear of darkness making light go away. If the light does go away the darkness comes. But as long as the light stays the darkness has no power to defeat it. There is nothing the darkness can do about it either.

Wind can blow light out if it is not properly organized. When this happens darkness can move in. Rain can dampen the holder of light so that it is no longer capable of being the vessel in which light can stay. Then darkness moves in. But darkness never can move into a place where light is. We are being philosophers now and are getting the philosopher's joy. This is an absolute truth: light is superior to darkness.

Well, no wonder that left the writer of Genesis

with nothing more to say for that day. It is a thrilling moment when you realize that you have a supreme truth at your fingers' ends. Quite properly Genesis records—"And the evening and the morning were the first day."

But going back to the idea with which we started this chapter, when you take life with the mind of the man on the street absorbed in the daily task, rather than the mind of the philosopher interested in abstract ideas, the great day for man was not the first but the fourth day.

Here is the meaning of the poet's fierce absorption in the infinite variety of finite forms, rather than the theologian's cool concern for infinite ideas. Life did not begin to make sense until man began to see the end of light, not its beginning; end in the sense not of cessation but of completion. The creation of light was an abstract fact. The organization of light—with sun to rule the day and moon to rule the night, and all the stars; and—if the poet who wrote the first chapter of Genesis had carried the idea a bit further—the organization of light into lamps, and hearths, and welding torches, and searchlights, and all the infinite varieties of its finite uses—that was the great day for man.

Now for the first time man sees the purpose of creation. This, he says, is the meaning and goal of light. Now it makes sense. "Then," to quote that gloomy-sounding but very honest and truly hopeful preacher of old Jerusalem, recorded in Ecclesiastes,

"Then I saw that wisdom exceedeth folly as far as light excelleth darkness." It was the evening and the morning of the fourth day.

Now, let's make concrete this difference between the first day and the fourth and the importance to the common people, which we are, in that fourth day. This is the day that Christianity has so often failed to reproduce.

Life has to rest on fundamentals, such as, to take our best example, on God. This is the beginning, and religion becomes a sentimentalism, emotional, frothy, unless you can carry it back to such a defensible frontier of faith. I know what life is like when a man does not believe in God. It loses all sense. It becomes a black and ugly thing. To continue to exist is often torment; to care about life or try to do anything about it is an absurdity. We say then with Hamlet, "How weary, stale, flat, and unprofitable, seem to me all the uses of this world! . . . 'Tis an unweeded garden, . . . things rank and gross in nature possess it." Of course! When the foundations have crumbled the superstructure crashes.

But the world will not be moved by its belief in God. It is the incarnation of God—the word made flesh and dwelling among us—which gives us power to become the sons and daughters of God. God was in the beginning. He is, symbolically speaking, the first day. Christ was the fourth day. As the light of the fourth day could not have been, if it had not also been existent in the fact of light in the first day, so

Christ was in the beginning with God. But the point which is important to us is that God was in Christ reconciling the world unto Himself. It is the realization of that specification of the light—or as John puts it, "The *life* was the light of men,"—which changes the lives of men.

Saul Kane, of John Masefield's *Everlasting Mercy*, an old friend but a good one to bear witness, is the spokesman at the moment. He was a dissolute young man, as bad as they make them. It is a good thing there were only ten Commandments; if there had been twenty he would have broken them too. Nobody could do anything with him. The idea of manhood, and what God thought, and all that, did not turn him a hair's breadth from his headlong way.

It was the little woman, who somehow cared for this hulk of a man and was neither afraid of nor for him, who finally got under his skin. She established that vivid sense of specific connection with a person when one night she knocked at his door and she told him straight out, "Saul Kane, when next you drink . . ." and by the miracle of her concern she makes him see in a flash of light his connection with all mankind. His sin is not his own. He has, by it, soiled every one.

Saul Kane stood there, conscious of his drunkenness, which, as he said, "shut out Christ in husks and swine." And suddenly the light became concentrated. It was given substance, form, finiteness, connection. Then there came the mystery of conversion.

The bolted door broke inward upon him. He sees in the "glory of the lighted mind" that:

> "Not alone we conquer,
> Not alone we fall,"

to use the words of an old hymn.

The end of light was to see itself becoming finite and useable form. It was not enough that "there be light." It must interpenetrate life's infinite, complex particulars.

Let us not miss the point in oversimplicity now. Some people think that they have caught the magic formula by calling upon the name of Christ, not seeing that men have sometimes taken Him away from men in their very attempt to give Him to them. The priest in Shaw's *Saint Joan* gives us a vivid picture of that:

He speaks to one of the courtiers about the cruel thing he had a part in doing to Joan because he had not understood the nature of cruelty. The tragedy of not knowing what cruelty means is that some one else has to endure suffering before you see for yourself.

The courtier asks the obvious, conventional question of why Christ's death was not enough to save him.

The priest replies that you would think Christ's suffering should be enough for any one. He had seen the pictures, had read the story, had been stirred emotionally to real feeling; or so he thought. Apparently, however, that had not made him understand the truth which had been obscured by the very glory the Church had given to the Christ. It was not until he saw the way in which Joan went to the stake that the priest understood Christ and was saved.

This makes his friend feel the awful sense of futility of a world with eyes which see not. Almost as a prayer from some tortured soul, he asks whether it must always be that every generation will require a Christ to perish in agony to save people who have no imagination.

Well, the answer is: Yes, a Christ must perish in every generation and for every man when the generation or the individual has not insight enough to create the form in which the light can be useful for the individual and the generation.

Here is one of the truly tragic facts about the life of man. It takes that seemingly infinite sacrifice of the good, the true, and the beautiful to save one person or any age which is so stupidly, inertly, blind to the light.

Even as we have gone back to the foundation in God and then have seen that life does not begin to make real sense nor take on dynamic direction until we see Him specified, made finite, incarnate, given form and substance, made flesh and dwelling among us as we have and do see it in Christ; so we can see it in another area of religious faith.

In the Epistle of John there is another of these absolutes:

"Beloved [John begins], now are we all the sons and daughters of God, and it doth not yet appear what we shall be: but we know that, when He shall appear, we shall be like Him; for we shall see Him as He is."

That is the first day of creation—the fact and appearance of light.

But what changes men? What makes them believe in this truth? It is seeing a man standing there, on the streets, side by side with you, who was a sinner and is now a saint, who was divided and is now whole, who was lost and is found, who was impotent and ignorant, who is now marvellously strong and wise.

Take a look at the record. How often Jesus answered the skeptic with the expression, "Come and see." "Go and tell what you have seen." "And seeing the man who was made whole, standing there, they could say nothing against it." Thus the record runs. It is the witness of life in finite form which gives men faith or doubt about the fact of light.

Either we hurt Christ's cause by standing in the way of man's desire to believe because they see we dare not live what we say; or we disturb the skeptical world by standing there as witnesses of a fact—that people do stand firm when the going is tough. By doing this we give to the world the witness, a very uncomfortable and strangely haunting witness, of people who find that to believe in Christ does make a man different—a difference which the world longs to believe it can have too.

For the world does not live by the first day. It lives by the fourth. Here are Charles and Barbara

in Galsworthy's *Worshipful Society* discussing Life
with a capital L. Charles says something about judging life by what he has seen. "By what you've seen,"
says Barbara, a little frantically. "If I went by what
I saw daily, hourly in the city we live in, I'd go mad
in a week." To which Charles soberly responds,
"But, Babs, what else can one go by?"

Well, let's not fool ourselves. Like it or not, that
is the way the world does judge: by what it sees.

You see, the testimony which may satisfy you and
me does not satisfy the world. For us, when we see
a person who professes Christ's way of life living an
un-Christlike life or doing an un-Christlike deed, we
console ourselves by saying that he is not a real Christian. I believe we are honest in explaining it that way.
But the unconvinced observers of our Christianity
are not touched at all by that answer. To be told that
this one, who does mean things in business, and that
one, who does mean things in personal relationships,
"is not a real Christian" seems to them to be dodging
the fact. Did not your Christ say, "By their fruits
ye shall know them"?

Look here, they put it to us with curious wistful-
ness, we have been interested in this Jesus you talk
about. But we are only human. We have the same
pressure for self, the same ambitious fears and hatreds,
the same environment to live in, the same limitations
of time, and space, and flesh. We cannot do what
you cannot do. Our major concern is what happens
to people like ourselves under the influence of this
religion-of-Jesus. But if your Christ after nearly 2000

years can only produce such *real* Christians as you, we are not sure we want to waste our lives on Him. If you in contact with the Church of Christ cannot stand against war and social injustice, if you cannot make a world where it is possible for people to have bread to eat, and work for their hands, and a dwelling place for their bodies-minds-and-spirits, which is not dark, damp, dirty, why ask us to accept your impotent religion?

We have to face that fact. It is not what happens on the first day when the truth was created, which affects the common man. It is what happens on the fourth day when we organize that truth into form and substance.

But also let us add quickly for our comfort that it is equally true—no, *more* than equally true—that the world cannot get over the fact of seeing a man standing in the world who lives without bitterness in a world sick with hate; who lives without fear in a world frantic with many fears; who refuses to accept defeat when he has apparently failed, because he believes that nothing is ever ended which is not ended right; who does not abandon a right cause even though it seems hopeless for the moment; who will not admit that a principle agreed to in the mind or conscience is defeated, because he knows that its triumph cannot ultimately be prevented.

You do not need to do more than give any man—note I said any man—half a chance, or for that matter any hopeful chance at all, to have him throw all his own interests into the balances for a cause. Without a quiver or a quaver he will do it, if he sees some one who believes an idea enough to stick with it to the end.

The tragedy of our Christianity is that the experience of the world may light upon you or me instead of some one who has stuck it out to the end. The world is like a man with bandaged eyes groping through life and judging what it is by what he touches. Suppose that man, hungry for the knowledge of a decent world, happens to lay his hands on you as he gropes. What would he think of Christ, if his hands happened to hold you as the witness of His Way?

It was something of this feeling, you older people will remember, which caught Samuels, the Jew, in Jerome K. Jerome's *The Passing of the Third Floor Back*. "He makes me feel uncomfortable," Samuels remarks about the Passer-by. "He said he trusted me 'because I am a Jew.' *Because!* What an idea! He trusts me *because* I am a Jew." Then the opportunity came to put over a slick deal. It was legal, but slick. Then Samuels remembers. He is surprised at himself, but sure. "I'm not going to sell the Jewish race," he said, "for one hundred pounds."

No! It is not worth it, whatever you gain. Like it or not, the world judges our light which comes from God and was proven in Christ; and the world judges God, who was revealed to us by Christ; and it sees our Christ as a possible Master and Leader, in what we do on the fourth day when the eternal truth was given finite and useable form.

This was the great day in creation: when the light

was organized. In the beginning God said, Let there be light. That was wonderful. But the test of creation came on the fourth day. On this, the fourth day of creation, what do you suppose people think about when they see how we have organized light in the world?

The end of light is not to "be," the end of light is to blot out all darkness that it may be said, wherever one holding the light stands, "there shall be no night there."

CHAPTER NINETEEN

And the Earth Moved

*I*F YOU have any sense at all and have lived long enough on this earth to have had some of its experiences all over again, you have been honest enough to say, at least to yourself, "What's the use! History is just repeating itself. The things which have been are those which will be. We are going around in circles. There is no new thing under the sun."

Part of that is from Ecclesiastes, which records an honest but somewhat disillusioned preacher in old Jerusalem. Part of it is what is in your minds, uttered or unexpressed as you look at the days of our years.

Unless you can face that question without losing your drive you are not going to be much help in the problem of this (or any) generation. Your life may light an altar, but will not alter a dark and windy world. We come back at the end to find out whether the question about the kind of light we have is an abstract or concrete reality.

We go back to the beginning of things and find that great Hymn to Creation saying, "In the beginning . . ." and then quickly follows a description of the earth, which even in these times seems still a good analysis: "The earth was without form, and void; and darkness was upon the face of the deep."

Then come the words: ". . . and the Spirit of God moved upon the face of the waters."

We are not being gloomy; we are only asking an honest question when we wonder sometimes where the evidence of that motion is. Why do we still believe there is motion, a purposeful and directed motion, to life? That motion, if it is at all, is to our eye imperceptible.

We feel with the psalmist who cries. "How long, O Lord, how long wilt Thou forget Thy people!" No wonder a man says sturdily but with a real need in his voice—this is from the Psalms: "Men laugh me to scorn." "They shoot out the lip, they shake the head, saying, He trusted in the Lord that He would deliver him. Let God deliver him, seeing he delighted in God." "They have opened their mouths wide against me saying, Aha, aha, our eye hath seen his plight."

Then comes in the Psalms a very satisfying line: "Arise, O Lord, and disappoint them." That is a great word—"disappoint" them. He does not ask for punishment upon a faithless and wicked generation—for God's wrath to be evidenced in fire and brimstone.

"Listen, Lord," man says in all simplicity. "Will you just show these people some day? That's all I ask. Let me stick around and watch them when they get that awful empty feeling inside of knowing that they were wrong about it all, all of this time. The Lord *doth* reign. He *is* Holy. The earth does *move*. 'Arise, O Lord, and disappoint them.' "

It is against such a background of natural feeling

that our closing chapter makes an assertion about what is oftentimes an imperceptible motion of life.

Realistically it *is* imperceptible. It takes a long look and a deep look to believe in progress in these days. We are flabbily sentimental unless we realize that.

But—life has a motion. It does make progress toward "that far-off divine event to which the whole creation moves." It is only those who believe this or who want to believe it who bother about going to church in days like these or who read books like this. And your usefulness to the beloved community of our hope depends a great deal upon whether you do believe it, really believe it in the pit of your being, or merely want to believe that life has a motion to it.

First of all we must be sure that it is from a real seeing of the world that we believe in motion. We can so easily be fooled by what we think we see. We take activity to be progress, not having penetration enough to see that. Activity and its private secretary, Statistics, may be only the management of a gaudier merry-go-round. The plaster horses may prance perpetually on their platform, bright with fresh red and yellow paint. The loudspeaker may send out with less scratching its slightly maudlin tune, "We're here, because we're here, because we're here, because we're here. . . ." Some people, drugged by superficial motion or drunk on percentages, may get an everybody's-happy feeling as they trace the trends through the comparative figures of the years and are content if the signs are toward progress. But it is not enough to satisfy us. You do not know whether you truly believe in life's motion until you have had the experience of the frictionless plane.

It was a high-school physics teacher with an imagination who first introduced me to that theoretical absolute of science. Upon a smooth steel plate he placed a thin film of light oil and in the center of that field he set down a long-legged bug. We watched it wriggle. There was plenty of action but no progress. Fast or slow, it made no difference; action or inaction, the bug stayed where he had been placed.

Like that, life seems sometimes. It makes you feel cold to the very pit of your stomach. Whether you do anything or not, life is what it is. Nothing you do or fail to do seems to change the course of the common life by a hair's breadth.

It is when life is in such a moment of awareness that you must decide what you truly believe about life's motion. It is in them that the value of a man's life is determined.

In that play by Maxwell Anderson, *Key Largo*, previously mentioned, the choice is set for us dramatically. We look now not at the almost melodramatic ending but at the decisions faced in the beginning. It opens with that group of American boys on a hilltop in Spain discussing their "cause." They believe it to be democracy's last stand. Whether they are right is not the point. They believe they are right as on that hilltop in Spain they do their bit for democracy.

Their cause is lost. They know that when their leader returns from the rear and tells them that Franco has won. Fighting now is but a mopping up. There is no military value in holding the line any longer. He tells them to cut the marks off their uniforms and to run for their lives.

They all set about it except one who quietly says that he is going to stay. With this boy, Victor, the leader, King McCleod, argues:

Victor: ". . . there is no God . . . the sky's
              quite empty,
              just as you said."

McCleod: "Then why do it? Why sit here
              and get yourself murdered? . . .
              You'll die for nothing. They'll walk
              right over you.
              Won't even pause."

Victor: ". . . I stay here to keep whatever it is
              alive that's alive inside me. . . .
              . . . there's something in the world that
              isn't evil—
              I have to believe there's something in
              the world
              that would rather die than accept
              injustice—
              . . . a man can die
              for what he believes—if ever the time
              comes to him
              when he's called to choose, and it just
              so happens
              it's up to me to-night.—And I stay here.
              I don't say it's up to you—I couldn't tell
              about another man—or any of you—
              but I know it's up to me.

. . . if I die
then I know men will never give in;
then I'll know there's something in the
      race
of men, because even I had it, that hates
      injustice
more than it wants to live.—Because
      even I had it—
and I'm no hero.—And that means the
      Hitlers
and the Mussolinis always lose in the end—
force loses in the long run, and the
      spirit wins,
whatever spirit is. Anyway it's the thing
that says it's better to sit here with the
      moon
and hold them off while I can. If I went
      with you
I'd never know whether the race was
      turning
down again, to the dinosaurs—this way
I keep my faith. In myself and what
      men are.
And in what we may be."[1]

Well, he died there—that boy. They walked right over him and didn't even pause, as the one who ran away to save his life said they would.

And the cynical world says: "You see? That's what it gets you—all these big ideas— Nothing. Don't be a dope? If there is any progress in the world—which

[1]Pp. 20 ff.

I'm inclined to doubt—you don't affect it any one way or the other. So listen, son: eat, drink, and be merry. You'll be dead a long time."

You have heard people say such things? Or do they just say them to people who make them feel uncomfortable because of believing so unwaveringly about this motion of life which is affected by what you, as an individual, do—or do not do?

Some day, time will take its measure of your life. Beside one of those boys somewhere in Spain, whatever your Spain may be, you will be found in the end.

There on the lonely hilltop of some cause the world says is lost, the flesh cries, "Run." Or better yet says, "Slip away. You can, you know. Just be not there any longer. After all, a man has a right to look out for himself."

Flesh says that? Well, Spirit says it too sometimes: this cause is lost. Give it up. Be sensible. Don't waste your life.

But what makes you feel decent? I do not need to tell you that. You will never forget a man who stays on the hilltop of a lost cause and lets them walk over him, if they must, but who stays there just the same.

That is why the world will never forget Jesus. There are a lot of people who wish He had never been born.

It is not because of His ideas. Men had argued about them before in learned dissertations and in "bull sessions." They would have argued about them again without Him.

I do not mean that His ideas were not important

or that He did not state them well. He did something to ancient truth which stuck it in men's minds. His vivid stories gave men unforgettable phrases. He painted pictures. He made of the life of the mind an illumination and a dynamic. He lighted men's minds with penetrating ideas.

But it was not the ideas of Christ which changed men.

The world has sometimes thought it was the ideas *about* Christ which change the world. Oftentimes, however, these have been only a respectable escape from the obligation of carrying His light. This does not mean that theology is not valuable. Without it I doubt if man would have come as far as he has. Through clear thinking on the how and why of life and of personality, men are released from confusions which web their wills and hold them impotent.

But it is not the doctrines—the dogmas or the creeds —about Christ which change men.

Men are affected by life

"Which looks on tempests and is never shaken;
Which alters not.when it alteration finds
But bears it out even to the edge of doom."

Shakespeare will have to pardon some transposition in the lines of one of his sonnets. The sense is as he put it.

This light of life, which Jesus said we were, is not "Time's Fool." Man's life on earth has value in proportion to his hope for, his understanding of, his allegiance to this motion of life which man has insight and will enough to serve.

I do not need to tell you, because rare is the person who has not experienced a loss of confidence in purpose, how one becomes at times what William Bolitho alliteratively described as "men motored by mere momentum." In those moments we sometimes go on, because we have been going on, and to stop is even more senseless than to keep on going.

But there is no thrust in life when we do, and quite trivial bumps can bring us to a stop. Institutions, and churches in so far as they let themselves become mere institutions with possessions and traditions as the major reason for their continuance, are often motored by mere momentum and are scarcely aware that they have lost their dynamic.

It is therefore worth while for us to have asked ourselves, as individuals and as parts of institutions, where our accent falls on the imperceptible motion of life and how our way of living has organized and made effective the light which shall some day "light it all where now it lights a part."

A group of young American climbers led by a medical student on their expedition to K^2, the next to the highest mountain of the earth, state the principle in words which I paraphrase.

We find them saying as they started out that they really did not expect they would reach the top. After all it had been tried only once before. Their job was to find the way by trying out different ways, some of which would prove impossible. Yet they knew that even if they were lucky enough to find without too much delay the way by which the mountain might be climbed, they probably would not have time enough left nor reserves of strength to reach the top. But they recalled the mountaineer's creed, that "men climb mountains on the shoulders of others." Some day some men, unhampered by having to explore and reject the impossible ways, would move directly on the possible way, which they or others after them had, by their failures and partial successes, discovered; and would stand at last upon the top. And when they do, all who went before can say, "In some measure this is our victory too."

These young men did say, when they returned from the unclimbed mountain, that of course every man secretly hoped that they would be the ones to reach the top. They would scarcely be human if they had not had that personal longing and desire to reach the top themselves.

But we have been touched by the quality of Jesus' spirit when we know, and pattern our lives on this we know, that through all the zig-zag, tick-tock, round-and-round motions of time, there is a motion perceptible to the spirit of man, which makes him unafraid to live and, if he must, to die for ideas which can be proven only by the giving of life.

A candle in the wind is not enough. We must be at the least a torch which goes not out. Our goal, however, is not the cross of martyrdom for an idea. Light is the principle of creation and we or others who follow us must learn how to use it to build at last Our Father's World.